Presented To:

Linda & Jocelyn

From:

Brenda Joyce Johnson

Date:

March 9, 2021

THE GET NOTICED WOMAN

Stand strong —
You a beautiful &
Valued!
Brenda L Johnson

THE
GET NOTICED
WOMAN

Brenda Joyce Johnson

Charleston, SC
www.PalmettoPublishing.com

First Edition

Printed in the United States

Paperback ISBN: 978-1-64111-630-5
eBook ISBN: 978-1-64990-635-9

ENDORSEMENTS

"*The Get Noticed Woman* is both timely and timeless. In a time when women's worth and rights are being questioned and even denied, Brenda Joyce Johnson's book is affirmation that in Christ, all women are worthy and beautiful. This book encourages every woman to reach beyond the surface, look within, be fearless, walk in her true purpose, and see who she REALLY is."

Trela Anderson, Ph.D.
Professional Writing Instructor
National Defense University
Washington, D. C

Readable, fascinating, and profoundly important. For eons there has been a stigma that dictates a woman's role in the family and in society. More significantly media standards for what a beautiful woman should look like, what designer looks to choose and how she should behave. Brenda shares biblical truths to expel misconceptions and untruths often accepted about women. She shares her own personal struggle with low self-esteem to lift our psyches to new levels of freedom, hope and purpose. The treasures I discovered in "The Get Noticed Woman" are life-changing.

Wilhemina Hall McKinney, Ed.D
Educational Consultant
Instructional Systems Specialist
Department of Defense Education Activity

Minister Brenda Johnson lays out so eloquently her years of expertise in the area of personal and professional development. *The Get Noticed Woman* is such an inspirational read for any woman at any stage in life. Not only are these pages full of wisdom and insight, but they are also filled with nuggets that will help women with self-confidence, image and their God-given potential. While reading this book, you become a student as she mentors you to be all you can be. It is definitely a must-read.

Patti Mellette, Co-Pastor
Christian Provision Ministries
Sanford, North Carolina

⌇⌐

If you are one of those accomplished but privately insecure women who need a refreshing place to tackle your secret fears about your true "self," while learning to appreciate your immeasurable value to the world, then *The Get Noticed Woman* is the read for you.

I found it to be an invaluable resource, providing realistic tools and guidance to confront private misconceptions surrounding the imagery of success, womanhood, and beauty that women strive so publicly to accomplish.

Lisa Goodman Age
Sergeant First Class, Retired
Doctoral Student, University of Phoenix

⌇⌐

ACKNOWLEDGEMENTS

AM GREATLY INDEBTED to my husband, The Rev. Dr. Lonnell E. Johnson for his love, patience and understanding as I labored for the last 18 months over the pages of this manuscript. I also thank him for his skillful hand as an editor.

I am especially grateful to my mentors and spiritual overseers. Many thanks to my brother, Apostle Eric Warren, whom I affectionately call, "big brother" (although he is 11 months and 3 weeks younger) and to his wife, Apostle Carolyn. He was the first to ordain me and to recognize the call of God on my life as a teacher. Thank you for your example, mentorship and for being a tower of strength to our family.

My second ordination came when I served under the leadership of Bishop Charles and Pastor Patti Mellette who entrusted me with a leadership role at Christian Provision Ministries in Sanford, North Carolina. Their oversight and example was healing and empowering.

This work would not have been completed without the professional skills of Debra Perry, Editor and Content Strategy Specialist. I also want to acknowledge with love and appreciation Rev. Stanley Reahard for her wise counsel, keen eye and editorial contributions.

My mother Rosa is my rock and forever cheerleader. Thank you mom for your prayers, songs of praise and heart for God that laid my spiritual foundation. I am grateful to my loving and precious dad whose namesake "BJ Warren" I carry with pride. To our daughter Melissa, her husband William and our little Kingston, you make Mimi's heart explode with pride and unending love. To Angela and her husband Shajuan—what a classy lady and teddy bear of a man. Your voices are music to my ears. Love you all forever.

To my brothers and sisters, Ross, Juanita, Mary, Glynn and Cynthia—I love you and am proud to be your big sister. To Barney, Jr. and Yvonne Warren, our dad loved family. We must allow that heart to continue. Our family has suffered the loss of four siblings, Phyllis, Shirley, Ruebin and Sylvester—you are forever etched on the tables of my heart with eternal love.

To every mentor and prayerful supporter of my many ministry projects, you are the wind beneath my wings. Thank you for your guidance, assistance and dedicated leadership. Together, we can change the world.

FOREWORD

DARK DAYS AHEAD! That's the warning I keep hearing. COVID deaths and pandemic plights of joblessness and school closings. But, women—take courage! I want to encourage you today. Did you know that the light shines brightest when days are dark? Hiding never works. When we carry the light—darkness is dispelled. When we embrace the power of Christ within, everything that moves must submit. Lights don't sink, they rise!

My grandson asked me a question before he was 4 years old. "Mimi, does the light chase the shadow?" Wow, I thought as I looked deep into his sunlit brown eyes--that's profound! His eyes were fixed on the shadows cast by our bedroom ceiling fan. Moments before, he asked about shadows. As he pointed to the ceiling, he said, "What's that?" I said, "That's a shadow." He said, "How do you make a shadow?" I said, "You can't have a shadow without light."

When God's kingdom comes—we have His will being done in the earth. We have light. My prophetic friend, Evangelist Evon, before she passed away, gave me a candle at my ordination. It said, "Light on assignment--Matthew 5:14-16." I often reflect on this scripture. The excellence of His glory is in us, when we proclaim His word. Yes, we chase the dark...consume and destroy the elements of its destructive power.

This truth continues to resonate in my very soul. For this reason, I take seriously my assignment to awaken women of faith to their God-given purpose and potential. For more than three decades, as an entrepreneur, educator, personal and spiritual mentor, image and etiquette coach and minister of the gospel, I intend to expose the tentacles of spiritual darkness that have imprison our minds. Lawlessness and discord have gripped our culture; however, God has always had a plan for redemption—and kingdom women, you are an intricate part of His plan for deliverance.

I've spent a life-time teaching soft skills, manners, and etiquette—relationship building skills that to some--now seem outdated and without merit. Superficial ideologies of social reform will not heal broken and wounded souls. Only God alone can transform the thoughts and intentions of our hearts. Only He can reveal hidden secrets and release us from our prisons. When we lock Him out, we block our ability to come together and heal. Dismissing pride and embracing change are the first steps required for transformation from the inside-out.

The Get Noticed Woman was written with a heartfelt-sensitivity to the yearnings of women who desire to function with a kingdom mindset and with spiritual integrity--with greater confidence and grace. It is designed for the woman who will readily embrace change. We were never created to be or become second-class citizens, relegated to a victim's mentality. Although women of faith have too often been sidelined and positioned in places of obscurity both inside and outside of the church, I believe the time comes in every woman's life when she must begin to arm herself with practical and spiritual knowledge in order to fulfill her God-given purpose. You do not need a title of Reverend or Elder to make an impact for the kingdom.

The word of God is the one and only true liberator from perceived limitations imposed by culture and society. At best, any other self-help book is inadequate. And guess what--hiding never works! I know because I've tried it. Neither does trying to live up to someone else's expectations. We must all report to the throne room of grace to get our marching orders. God has fortified our wombs to birth nations and to nurture greatness. We cannot circumvent His instructions and live without consequence. How can we produce and nurture healthy progeny, when we ourselves are fractured and broken?

Each chapter of this book was written to inspire and encourage—to help strengthen women of God in our everyday functions as daughters, wives, parents, pillars in our communities and more. Our voices and value matter as we partner with our Creator to be His lights in dark places.

The Get Noticed Woman is designed to provide practical tools for promotion and advancement—not just spiritually but, guidelines to help navigate through life with finesse, wisdom, and class. Life can present challenging situations we must all face. When a young girl or a mature woman feels inadequate, her world begins to crumble. The guidance provided in *The Get Noticed Woman* will help women present their very best as ambassadors for Christ.

Tenacity and touch-mindedness is required to endure hardships of the COVID pandemic. Women with fearless faith who know how to persevere with prayer can be victorious during this hour. We must not and cannot bow to manipulation and intimidation. I consider this my current life's mission—to lay a foundation for strengthening next- generation leaders who fearlessly follow Christ—without apology.

Adam named Eve "life-spring," because she was the mother of all living. Even as God chose to bestow prominence and dignity to womankind in the beginning, He will still be our partner today as we listen to the voice of destiny calling. For this reason, I am encouraging kingdom women to join me in "the awakening" of women of faith. As lights in a dark world, we are called to place our lights on a lamp stand. Let's chase the dark. As His light-bearers, let's be tenacious and purposeful about drawing men and women to Him. It's time to—get noticed!

INTRODUCTION

G OD CREATED TWO genders, Adam and Eve—male and female and blessed them. Eve, the first woman became the *mother of all living.* God made her a queen—the monarch of a kingdom. As was true with Queen Esther, she reigned with preeminence because her name means "star." With God-inspired revelation and wisdom, she submitted her life to prayer, using her wit, wisdom, and influence to squash a demonic plan to exterminate the people of God.

Our culture and society need pillars of excellence who stand tall--out and above all the noise as a lighthouse in a world of chaos and confusion. Our prayer life and walk of faith are keys to kingdom living--drawing others to Him.

Is it not true, that kingdom women—just as Queen Esther are stars and light-bearers for all to see God's glory, majesty, and beneficence? Who has deceived us and misnamed us, causing today's kingdom woman to reside in hidden places? Is it possible that the prisons within which we reside are actually bars of captivity erected by self-doubt and failure to believe? The King of glory desires to release us to be salt and light to a dying world.

Whom do you know who would intentionally hide a light? No one desires to partake of tasteless food. As God's light-bearers, we must use our talents and anointing from the Holy Spirit to reveal the secrets of God's heart, so that those who choose His Word can be released from prisons of their minds.

Our date of birth, the numbers of hair on our heads, and the purpose for which He created us are most certainly known by our Heavenly Father. But do you know your significance and why He created you to occupy space on our planet at this particular time in the history of the world? Whose lives you are to impact? How might you make a difference to bring peace and harmony where discord resides and healing is needed?

Matthew 5:14 states that kingdom men and women are the lights of the world. It also says that together, we are a city that cannot be hidden. We are encouraged and admonished to let our light *so* shine—so there can be no doubt He resides within us of a truth. The ultimate result will be that our good deeds will bring praise and honor to our Heavenly Father. This is very little to ask for the sacrifice He gave at Calvary.

At this moment, race wars, numerous health crises, global chaos, political discord, rebellion against civil authorities, and religious hostilities threaten our peaceful co-existence. The Get Noticed Academy, LLC is training Titus II mentors to uphold and sustain our biblical heritage as women of faith. As you read the following pages, I am praying that you will become even more energized to put on the whole armor of God, so that you may stand in the evil day.

My prayer, also is that you will begin to ask God for deeper revelation into His purpose and will for your life. Women represent approximately half of the human race. As God's light-bearers, we want to be all He has called us to be. We want to make a difference. When we have all the tools and keys we need to live with confidence and excellence, we can soar. May you be enlightened and encouraged as you read the *Get Noticed Woman.*

TABLE OF CONTENTS

CHAPTER ONE

IDENTITY CRISIS

TO ALL MY women friends with bright eyes and an insatiable zeal for life. Who are you today? Are you a wife, mother, grandmother, minister, parent, counselor, CEO, doctor, educator, student, wife, mom, grandmother or caregiver? I'm sure it just depends upon what day of the week or the time of day you are asked.

None of us really likes labels because sometimes they engender more questions than answers. Once we share our personal or professional status or title, more queries ensue causing us to question why we were asked in the first place.

Our roles as women have caused more questions and controversy than any of us want to discuss or admit. Since the 60s, women have been told that they can "bring home the bacon, cook it up in a pan and never let you forget you're a man…" Hmm, now that's a pretty tall order. I can hear my four-year-old grandson commenting (without knowing why) … "How cool is that!"

Perhaps, like me, you've heard many sermons and motivational coaches who remind us that we "have it all," we can "be anything we set our minds to!" The problem is, they don't hang around long enough to walk us through the detailed process of accomplishment.

So, who are you today? And even more important, who or what are you seeking to become?

Today's woman is different. She wants to do more and be more. Because of the many conversations I've had with women over the years, I know that one thing hasn't changed: women are apprehensive about their future. As before, they are still feeling that somehow, their best isn't quite good enough. Women continue to have concerns about how they appear to others. They wonder, "Is my body fit? Are the kids getting enough attention?" They also wonder if the career they worked so hard to acquire is really bringing the satisfaction they deserve.

All these concerns and more continue to nag at her brain and grab her focus. Rather than feeling self-assured and confident, she feels more comfort in pretending she's really ok.

Self-identity is powerfully impacted by our thoughts, feelings and emotions. We can become confused when we find disparity between who we want to be and have become as opposed to false expectations placed upon us.

I recently had a conversation with a lady I am mentoring. She hadn't had a vacation in six years. She is single with no dependents and extremely focused on getting the job done. She prided herself in being a hard worker and extremely efficient and dedicated. She was working 6 days a week and had taken on volunteer work in addition to holding an assignment in her church.

Something else I noted was that she found it difficult to be honest with her boss to say that his expectations were unrealistic. She finally came to the realization that what she had identified as being "a hard worker" could more accurately be called "self-imposed slavery."

Times of self-evaluation are important for all of us. The truth is that women are often stretched beyond capacity. We find ourselves carrying an unreasonable amount of the household and workplace burden. Sometimes out of necessity and sometimes out of a need to feel useful and involved, we overcommit.

Because we are many times, overextended and exhausted, we can also show signs of being unhealthy. According to Statista.com, approximately 24% of American women experience a diagnosable mental health disorder compared to 15% of men. We also disproportionately experience heart disease, depression, panic and eating disorders.

The Get Noticed Woman is for the woman of God who wants more. She will not settle for mediocrity. She wants more for herself, her family, her community, her place of worship, culture and society.

Let's take a journey toward self-awareness and self-discovery. Let's talk about our identity as women. No matter what role we have been assigned or "accidently" fallen into, at some point we need to figure out who we really are and what we want. Sure, our children call us "mom," and our business card gives us a title and sense of identity, but, at one point or another in life, we must ask ourselves—"When God placed me in the earth for such a time as this, what assignment did He have in mind?" What was God's dream? How would he have me to fulfill my God-ordained purpose?

The complexities and confusion in our lives often lies in the demands our family, places of worship, communities, etc. places upon us. We must then evaluate our personal values, as well as what our priorities are to be according to God's word. Finally, we must certainly consider what we believe to be our God-ordained mission and purpose personally, professionally and spiritually.

I am always fascinated with Jeremiah 1:5 which states:

> *I knew you before I formed you in your mother's womb...*
> *I knew you and set you apart...*

How amazing to find there is a "pre-plan" God has for our lives! We all know that the first 7-to-10 years of our lives are critical to identity and ideology. Those years fundamentally shape the way we think and behave even in our adult life. What values do our family hold dear? How are we told to view ourselves and how are we taught to view others? What is the education level and exposure of our parents? The answers to these questions shape, mold and build the identity we will finally embrace as our own. As young adults, we must distinguish between the values that hold true and those that do not.

WHAT WILL I ACCEPT OR REJECT?

For most of us, our families exposed us to both acceptable and unacceptable ideals to live by. This was and should continue to be a good thing. However, today's culture, laced with social media images, name-calling and just plain rudeness has introduced us to a whole new level of crude and unacceptable messaging and behavior.

I recently listened to an expert on teen sex and porn addiction. He warned teachers, professionals and parents that it is important to understand that purchasing your child a cell phone is not as innocent as purchasing a new pair of jeans.

He shared that when parents purchase a cell phone or tech device for their children, they might do well to also give them a sex education lesson as well. He explained that the internet targets young people and teens enticing them with information, photos, and toys that would even make adults blush. He also explained that googling an innocent word can open up whole new worlds of porn and introduce them to movies and songs that are designed to stimulate their curiosity.

The facts are alarming. The pornography industry generates $12 billion dollars in annual revenue. This is more than the revenues of NBC, CBS and ABC annually. Because of the vulnerability of our youth, we must as parents, grandparents, educators and ministry leaders sound the alarm so that our communities, non-profits, churches and educational institutions are aware of this menacing threat to our culture and society. For more information see: The Porn Industry Archives—Enough is Enough.

Daily and hourly, sexual predators are trolling the internet looking for unsuspecting youth to prey upon.

As many of us know, exposure to pedophilia and seductive sexual images can cause addictive behaviors leading to mental health disorders, sexual identity crises and unhealthy behaviors lasting a life-time.

Being well informed is one of the responsibilities of parenting. Identity confusion begins with some of the subtle exposures presented everyday—many times going unnoticed. Protecting our hearts (minds and thoughts) can be challenging enough for adults. All the more, unsuspecting children are impressionable and quick to embrace what they see and hear.

When our morals, personal and spiritual convictions are challenged, we must find guidance. Colossians 2: 8 provides a clear warning and a word of wisdom that I believe is appropriate to mention here.

Colossians 2:8 (NAS): See to it that no one takes you captive through philosophy and empty deception, according to the tradition of men, according to the elementary principles of the world, rather than according to the principles of Christ.

IDENTITY MISCONCEPTIONS

Webster's describes an identity crisis as a state of confusion regarding one's role and what's expected of us. This state of mind can impact us on a personal psychosocial level; as well as impact our lives in the spirit.

There is no question that women are often perplexed and at odds with how we can and should perform juxtaposed to certain expectations. Our personal and professional lives demand obligations we sometimes view as unreasonable. Even on a spiritual level, activities connected with our places of worship require our talents and attention. The demands seem unending. The reason parenting can seem overwhelming is because children often reflect the insecurities of their parents.

Functioning without certainty as to who we are, why we are here and for what purpose is frustrating both mentally and physically. When we have questions about how our lawn mower is to function, we go to the manufac-turer's manual. Because there are so many voices clamoring for our atten-tion, the wise thing for kingdom women to do is to seek wisdom and answers from our Creator. The word of God is a reliable source to find guidance and instruction. I have found comfort and clarity from Jeremiah 29:11:

For I know the plans I have for you, declares the Lord. Plans to prosper you and not to harm you, plans to give you hope and a future.

This verse reminds us that God had a dream in mind when he created humankind. Ladies, this includes us. We weren't left out. This tells us that from the beginning, God had a preordained plan to give us hope and a future. This plan, however, had a contingency requiring us to listen to and follow the instructions he gives in his word.

The structure he designed beginning in Genesis was good and perfect. He gave man and woman a role. God's plan provided not only companionship for the two of them, but this union would produce progeny which would extend his goodness and blessings to countless generations.

Unfortunately, most often, when we read Jeremiah 29:11 it is not read in context. God gives instructions to the elders, priests and prophets in the Old Testament. Here he outlines the foundational standards and structure for culture and society for his people under the rule of Nebuchadnezzar.

Although God's people were in captivity, he made sure his priest and prophets taught them how they should live. They were given the following instructions:

- Build houses, plant gardens and eat the fruit of them.

- Take wives and birth sons and daughters. Give wives for your sons and give your daughters to husbands.

In addition, although their captors would be considered enemies, they were to seek the peace of the city and pray for it. In praying for the city, they would have peace. Within these parameters, we can find our role as a woman, our hope, future, prosperity—and even our peace.

Of course, since the fall of man in the garden, culture and society have been at odds with the plan of God. Even kingdom women and men rebel and believe (by our actions) that God's plan and process simply doesn't work. So we've adopted alternative lifestyles and constructed our own paradigms and "liberties" to suit ourselves.

When I have discussions with women of God today, I find that they listen to and are informed by prominent voices, ideologies and political agendas. Because the women they most admire do not always use the word of God as their standard for faith and practice, the blind lead the blind. The deceptive tactics of false Gods lead to unanswered questions, doubt and confusion.

Understanding faith-based truth requires study of the scriptures. The disciples of Jesus were not blind followers, but, disciplined ones. We too, as his disciples are to be followers of his word and example.

So, why do believers live with uncertainty, lacking confidence and direction? As we study this topic, we will find that the identity crisis facing today's kingdom woman is birthed in *misplaced values*. Too many foreign and familiar voices snuff out our passion for prayer, praise, purity and submission to the wisdom offered in the word of God. There is an amazing scripture in Psalm 34:10 reminding us:

Young lions lack food and go hungry, but those who seek the Lord will not lack any good thing.

If the word of God is indeed true, this scripture is telling us that if we have need in our lives—we are lacking because we haven't sought the Lord. So, how do we do this?

One way is prayer and praise. Read the Psalms. This was King David's saving grace. He was by no means perfect, but, he was a man after God's own heart. Why? He had an intimate relationship with God. He was all in—not just in word, but his heart was true to his God. We are reading today the sentiments of his heart in true worship to his faithful God.

Of course, today, we want to appear to be "relevant." We don't want to appear to look like fossils with our heads stuck in the ground when we speak of our faith. We don't want to sound archaic and out of touch. However, woman of God, allow me to speak clearly. We must abandon the fear of not being accepted and misunderstood. The fulfillment of our future hopes and dreams is dependent upon our ability to dismiss the opinions of others. We must determine to adjust our thinking and lifestyles to comply with the word of God.

Observing God's plan brings amazing and miraculous results. Misunderstanding the privilege God gives us to live and breathe introduces darkness into our lives rather than the light and beauty of life. Current "thought leaders" have taken the liberty to redefine and repurpose God's original plan. Rather than the model taught in Jeremiah 29, where a man partners with his wife to bring forth children, we see a whole new paradigm embraced.

Our culture and society is changing rapidly. When women today speak of their "identities"—even in the faith community, we find that they may be referring to a multiplicity of genders and lifestyles. A plethora of choices have been introduced, unfounded by scripture. Open "marriages" and homosexual lifestyles with no marriage at all have become prevalent. We daily contend with contemporary ideologies and terminology like, reproductive and abortion "rights" under the banner of human rights.

If we truly believe God created us male and female—he would not be all wise and all-knowing had he not also provided a plan, purpose and design for our lives. As kingdom women, we understand that his plan will never hurt us, but, usher in a sense of joy and fulfillment. Although attitudes regarding bearing children have become widely diverse and controversial—God says they are a blessing.

Ask yourself this: If I have the ability to bear children, is this a "right" or is it a privilege? Did God enable childbearing for matters of convenience or affordability? We must evaluate and question current attitudes, political statements and sociological constructs. Do they reflect and mirror the standards revealed in scripture?

Another question, do we have the "right" to terminate or to abort a child in the womb? The real question is this—do we have the right to take the life of a living soul? Because God marks us as his own—numbering even the hair on our head, we are being more than presumptuous when declare, "My body, my choice?" What about the "right" to reassign (change) the biological gender God gave us at birth?

Of course, we all have *freedom* by choice and often by law to do these things. We can choose to take a life—or to spare a life. However, once we are born again, scriptures tell us we were bought with a price. Our lives are no longer our own. For this reason, we are admonished to glorify God in our bodies. As kingdom women, we observe the wisdom of God, knowing that as the Apostle Paul said in John 17:16: My doctrine is not mine, but his that sent me…"

The word of God is rich with examples of "get noticed" women who did not compromise—but stood strong on standards of truth. That's why their lives stand out from the pages. Ruth, Esther, Elizabeth, Mary, Lydia and more. They show us the way to think, speak and behave—simply by their manner of life. For this reason, God's word becomes our primary source of faith and practice as the very best resource to enhance and empower our personal and professional lives.

Social movements that attempt to speak for "voiceless women" have come and gone. As a young woman, I witnessed the flower children of the 60s who marched in protest for social injustice by burning their bras. Today, feminist rally for racial justice, equal pay, abortion "rights" and more. Nothing has really changed. Social unrest, consistent chaos and confusion in the streets are the symptoms of lost hope and prevailing fear. The moral foundations and fabric of what is meant to be a stable society has become almost threadbare. Somehow, I think we know we've lost our way.

In the U.S., adults are opting to delay marriage and even avoid it altogether. In a study done in 2019, Pew Research reports that in recent years, in the age group of 18 to 44, cohabitation has risen from 3% to 7%. For the first time ever, adults who have lived with an unmarried partner is now higher than those who have ever been married. Attitudes have shifted on morality and the family. Couples are opting for same sex relationships and sex for recreation rather than commitment. Even Christian couples have given up on basic tenets of the faith.

I've discovered that self-appointed leaders who speak their truth out of pain and disappointment have caused me to ask myself a question. Since I have a relationship with the creator of the universe, why not ask him to give me the courage and impetus for me to raise my voice to speak the truth that is in God's word. Scripture, is packed with "get noticed" examples where women of God turned chaos and panic into peace.

Esther was one of those women. With God's help, she was able to save her people from genocide by hiding her identity so that she would survive a "racist" society. The woman we famously have named in Christianity, "the Proverbs 31 Woman" carried out her role as a wife and entrepreneur with excellence. We too must seek God, asking him to impart wisdom, so that we can impact our homes and culture in a definitive way.

The example of Mary, the mother of Jesus is unparalleled. When faced with shame, humiliation and death, she declared, "Be it unto me according to thy word." It is comforting to have peace and know that everything will be well. Yet, this requires living with the faith that God is sovereign and believing the answer to every dilemma will be there—right when we need it.

So, with whom do you identify? Is it with those who attempt to make a difference by using tools of division and destruction? I encourage you to choose to study the examples of biblical heroines who chose to consult with the Creator of all life before speaking or acting rashly. Your choices not only impact you, but future generations. When we are confident about our identity, we need only to make but one statement. "Jesus you are Lord!" Those who hear His voice will see, hear and follow.

YOU'RE NOT JUST A PRETTY FACE

Women the world over are known for their beauty. Shania Twain and R.J. Lange wrote a song called, "She's Not Just a Pretty Face." I love this song because it expresses my heartfelt feelings about women and how we should choose to think and feel about ourselves. It's featured on her CD "Up!" where Twain suggests that women face so much adversity—it can only go "up" from here. You know it—and so do I.

Life can crush and even devastate us to the point of desperation. Yet, why not take this positive approach to life? If you're not familiar with this song, be sure to Google her and enjoy her contemporary, upbeat sound with a country flavor.

Do me a favor, as you listen to the song, take pride in knowing that your role as a woman is not limited to baking cookies and passing out fans in the choir stand at church. God has given many of us gifts and talents to be utilized within and outside of our home and local churches. Have intimate conversations with your Creator. Get that paintbrush and canvas out of the attic or enroll in that acting course at the community college. We've got potential and God's got an assignment for us to do.

She's Not Just a Pretty Face

"She hosts a TV show—she rides the rodeo. She plays the bass in a band. She's an astronaut—a valet at the parking lot—a farmer working the land.

She is a champion—she gets the gold. She's a ballerina—the star of the show."

Chorus: "She's not just a pretty face—she's got everything it takes. She has a fashion line—a journalist for "Time"—coaches a football team."

"She's a geologist—a romance novelist. She's a mother of three. She is a soldier, she is a wife. She is a surgeon; she'll save your life."

Chorus: "She's not just a pretty face; she's got everything it takes. She's mother of the human race..."

I'm wondering if there is a career choice named in this song that you abandoned or gave up on due to the overwhelming challenges you faced. My prayer is that "The Get Noticed Woman" will inspire you to reclaim the courage to do and to be all that you desire to be. Identity is reflective. You become what you see *in God's mirror.* That is why you must stay prayerful and be selective with your associates and mentors. What we hear, see and listen to will significantly impact our feelings and attitudes regarding self-identity.

Do not allow yourself to be limited by what others think your role in life should be. Confusion about your identity is often the result of misinformation, trauma, negative people and messages. Listening to the wrong messages and entertaining degrading thoughts is counterproductive. You must intentionally renew your thinking to awaken the giant that lies within.

One pebble in a brook will make waves that are far-reaching. What you believe about you has a way of cascading—impacting and influencing others. That's the way God planned it. His desire was to impart goodness and greatness into each life so that our influence would make a powerful impact and prevail.

For those of us who have read Genesis 2:25, we know that before the fall of Adam and Eve; they were naked, yet, had no shame. They were flawlessly created by their Creator and felt no sense of lack. They were his masterpiece. After their disobedience in the garden of Eden, we find the two of them hiding because their disobedience had caused guilt and shame.

The feelings of inadequacy, lack and a misplaced identity have unfortunately been passed down to the rest of us. We are still hiding behind the guilt of past sins, misguided Bible teachings, trauma and abuse. For this reason, our quest as kingdom women, to be mentally free is ongoing.

Once we accept Christ as Lord, our point changes. We now understand that we've been elevated to a position of authority in Christ. By choice, we are no longer conformed to this world— but, are transformed into the image of His son. We are called His "holy and beloved." We are now clothed with new nature.

Colossians 3:12:
Therefore, as the elect (specifically chosen for a purpose) of God, holy and beloved, put on tender mercies, kindness, humility, meekness, long suffering..."

Why should we feel inferior when the king of glory, by way of the Holy Spirit specifically calls us his "elect?" What does it matter—the size of our body, length of our hair or the color of our skin? The word of God empowers us so that we can become more authentic and confident about our identities as kingdom women.

Yes, before you had eyes that could see—or ears that could hear—God had a dream, packaged in a particular body, with a unique personality. She would be born at a particular time and in a particular place. Her parents would give her a name and she would make a unique contribution to her family, community and world. Her influence would mark a place in time and fill a space that belongs only to her. That person is you.

Psalm 139:13 ...You covered me in my mother's womb. I will praise you; for I am fearfully and wonderfully made...my substance (bone) was not hid from you when I was made in secret...

Your eyes did see my substance, yet being without perfection; in thy book all my members were written ...before they came into existence.

How precious also are your thoughts unto me, O God! How great is the sum of them!

The word "covered" in Psalm 139:13 means to be "hedged in." It's as if God is saying, "I've got you protected and covered." Just think of how we as women make decisions to interrupt the nurturing process of a baby before birth. I know, for all the "right" reasons we would say. But, remember that God's thoughts and ways are not like ours. Yes, there is forgiveness for wrong decisions, however, have we stopped to think how impactful it would be to consider his thoughts first, before we make life-altering decisions? God was so thoughtful about us, that he has a book where He chose to write all our members. Just like the snowflake He crafted, our identities are distinct and notable.

Our daughter, Melissa, has a brand identity program to help equip women mentally, emotionally and professionally define what makes them unique. This place of self-discovery will lead them to a powerful place of accomplishment in the business arena. She shares with her clients that their identity marker is their DNA: Distinct—Notable—Asset. They cannot be duplicated, replicated or copied. They are authentically unique and special within their own right. When they put their minds to it, their dream can become a reality. I use this confidence builder in my training exercises:

Excellence can be achieved if you...
Care more than others think is wise
Dream more than others think is practical
Expect more than others think is possible
Risk more than others think is safe
Do more than others think is reasonable

Another powerful way to upgrade your skills is to work with an accountability partner. Personal, spiritual and professional mentors help women bridge the gap between what is desired and how to reach meaningful goals. I once heard a personal growth expert say that we need at least 3-5 mentors or accountability partners to overcome personal, financial and mental health challenges.

The key to advancement in our personal, professional and spiritual lives is to be intentional about addressing our insecurities and short-comings before we reach the crises stage. Sometimes, women hire an image or branding coach to help them manage what they believe to be deficits in personality, appearance and confidence. They are intentional about overcoming bad habits and want to rise above perceived inadequacies to stand out in exceptional ways.

It is also important to understand that youth being brought up in a broken home or having to face significant trauma when growing up can cause enormous psychological and emotional set-backs. A report I recently read states that teenagers in single-parent families and blended families (which was my case) are three times more likely to need psychological help within a given year. (Peter Hill "Recent Advances in Selected Aspects of Adolescent Development" Journal of Child Psychology and Psychiatry 1993). This was my truth.

Another statistic I read while surfing the internet states that seventy percent of long-term prison inmates grew up in broken homes. (Horn, Bush, "Fathers, Marriage and Welfare Reform). Although I was never a law-breaker or found myself incarcerated, it is chilling to look at these statistics and think this could have been my plight.

My mother never would have dreamed that her marriage would end in divorce the first time—nor that her second marriage would be worse. However, this was her truth. Like many women today, her circumstances left her feeling helpless. I don't think we know enough about the impact of growing up in an unstable home or the impact of divorce.

As adults, it is good to know that we can advance beyond our past. Making the choice to overcome our fears and inhibitions is a step in the right direction. My advice to those desiring to upgrade in any category of life—as well as to capture your true identity would be to:

- Find ways to discover what qualities make you distinct and notable. Ask a friend or colleague to share what they've observed and write down what is said.

- Note the compliments that continue to surface. Write down what you remember.

- Capture the notable qualities that were mentioned by others as well as what you remember. Practice the presence of God. Go to him in prayer asking him to open doors of opportunity to help you develop your aptitudes and skills.

- Invest time and your finances to upgrade your skills. This means educating yourself by reading, enrolling in online courses and programs.

- Finally, look for opportunities to utilize your skills to enhance the lives of others.

THE CIRCLE OF LIFE

Life offers reciprocal opportunities of ebb and flow. The *Lion King* is a movie that was released by Disney in 1994. It is a children's musical of an epic tale bringing to life the reality of how little Simba the lion grows up and learns about manhood from his dad, Mufasa. The villain of the movie is Mufasa's jealous brother, Scar, who orchestrates a stampede. In a vicious and ruthless move of hostility, he pushes his brother off a steep mountain to his death. Scar's last words to his brother before this fatal move was, "Long live the king." This, of course, was a sarcastic and heartless comment filled with hate and revenge. Nevertheless, because Mufasa had progeny, his life, legacy and influence would live on.

No truer words were spoken. When God saw fit to initiate your birth, he had a dream to make you a queen. Although the enemy brings adversity into our lives, designed for your demise, God has a prevailing plan to bring us to prominence in his circle of life. If you are familiar with the story of the Lion King, you know that baby Simba became "the lion king" after his father's death.

Once we become a child of God, our identities are irrefutable. We are now a child of the king and an heir of His promises. Just as with Simba, we are on a journey of discovery. He was continually looking, learning and growing into his final purpose—to become king. The reality of his heritage and birthright could not be erased. This truth and its application in our own lives can be understood by reading Romans 8:29-30:

For those God foreknew, he also predestined to be conformed to the likeness of his Son that he might be the firstborn among many brothers. And those he predestined, he also called; those he called, he also justified; those he justified, he also glorified.

What, then, shall we say in response to this? If God is for us, who can be against us?

Reading this and the rest of Romans chapter 8 brings clarity, helping us understand God's dream for us in the spirit. Seed in the natural and in the spirit is sacred—and when it comes forth, it is already packaged and prepped with potential. We were prepped by God to succeed. We belong to him and what belongs to God, belongs to us. We are his masterpiece created in Christ Jesus for good works.

When we identify with him by accepting him as Lord, we become a co-partner with him in the kingdom to fulfill his plan for the earth. We are the manifestation of his dream birthed into time and space for such a time as this. For this reason, we must master the art of investing in ourselves—and then, make it a practice to give back to others. This is the power of influence and advancement. This is the power of our inheritance at work—God making himself known in the earth!

My second ordination occurred on December 6, 2015 at Christian Provision Ministries in Sanford, North Carolina where Bishop Charles and Pastor

Patti Mellette are overseers. My friend, Minister Yvonne Hughes, who is now deceased, gave me an unforgettable gift that night. It was a candle with the inscription: "Light on Assignment: Matthew 5:14-16." I cherish this candle always, because it spoke to my calling and destiny—my spiritual identity. If you are born again, you too are a "Light on assignment." Let's read what the word of God says about us.

"You are the light of the world. A city set on a hill cannot be hidden......it gives light to everyone in the house. In the same way, let your light shine before men, that they may see your good deeds and praise your Father in heaven."

Our identity, distinctiveness, individuality and uniqueness is made known as we manifest the brilliance and effulgence of Christ. We are a light on assignment in the earth. As salt and light, we were meant to heal and bring hope. Salt preserves, adds flavor and light illuminates. If we do not know the strength of our power, or the magnitude of our value and worth, then, the word of God explains to us that our lives become essentially useless in the earth.

When we understand our identity in Christ, we can become a beacon of hope to those who stumble in darkness. We bring spice to life—adding meaning and purpose to a "tasteless" lackluster existence. Christ died to bring restoration—to heal the breach between God and fallen mankind. The Christ in us was meant to bring hope to the hopeless and answers to those who are lost and confused.

"Nothing can dim the light which shines from within."
–Maya Angelou

The "get noticed woman" stands out and above the crowd because she is convinced that her identity has a heavenly origin. The totality of its essence cannot be captured on a business card—nor will we be able to find adequate words for our tombstones. The life we live should give honor and credit to our Creator. Our legacy should be satisfactory evidence that he is still alive—because of the victories we've won and the lives we've changed.

A FORMULA FOR CHANGE

To unleash transformation in our personal, spiritual or professional lives, we must act decisively to change our habits. Dr. Wayne Schmidt, a senior pastor at Kentwood Community Church in Grand Rapids, Michigan, created this formula which you will find helpful as you pursue change in your life. It's based on the premise that people with a passionate desire to change their lives, must acquire a strong sense of dissatisfaction.

$D + V + F + R$

D = A Dissatisfaction is the first state of mind required for a person to want to do something different. (For many people, this translates into being "stuck in a rut.")

V = A Vision is required to determine how you want things to be. (What do you envision for your personal appearance and how are you building relationships with your image and etiquette skills?)

F = First Steps toward change requires a commitment to take action. (Plot an easy-to- manage plan of action; i.e., I will read and apply one etiquette principle each day.)

R = Resistance to change is inevitable. Where there's no resistance, there's no change! (Welcome and expect resistance to your action plan. Commit to meet each challenge head-on. Ask for strength and resolve to carry out your vision.)

Change is challenging, but, you can do it! Expect resistance. I think sometimes the reason we are not successful during times of transformation is that we pray and expect miracles to automatically happen. Being tough minded and resilient is essential. Oftentimes, things will get tougher before they get better.

Your journey is just beginning and I am anxious to reveal insider secrets used by professionals like myself, to enhance your personal, social, and business life. Let's dig deep into the word "beauty" to begin to reveal the essence of a more captivating and influential you!

CHAPTER TWO

THE BEAUTY MYSTIQUE

WHAT IS BEAUTY to you? Do you have it? Do you believe this quality is available to some and not to others? As we begin to unveil the complexities of being and becoming a confident and classy kingdom representative, let's look at the term "beauty." In my experience, women often feel more comfortable discussing the word "attractive" rather than the concept of being "beautiful." Why is this? Perhaps, this is because, as women, we may feel more comfortable discussing our personalities or the compliments we've received. After all, we might think, "I certainly don't want to reveal how I really feel—or speak too highly of myself, giving the wrong impression."

We can all agree that the term "beautiful" has complex and diversified meanings depending upon who we talk to. Most of us, however, think of a beautiful person as one who is attractive, confident and has the ability to make others feel comfortable around them.

So, why does this word cause anxious thoughts and discomfort? I've often wondered about this and believe that this is because the term "beautiful" is quite controversial—no matter how we choose to define it. As we explore our feelings, I believe we will all agree that there are explanations for what we believe—which impacts our thoughts, attitudes and behavior.

Our perception of ourselves and others is predominantly rooted in the values and attitudes displayed by our family members, friends, faith communities with which we associate and more. In addition, our education, ethnicity, as well as the community we live and grew up in are also important considerations. As we connect with family, friends and associates, we are consistently picking up "vibes" and even comments that leave us with certain feelings and impressions.

FRAGILE BEGINNINGS

My upbringing included roadblocks, as well as stepping-stones that led to my transformation from being a shy, introverted little girl, to a young woman hungry for knowledge and exploration. I was taught the importance of good grooming, but, I don't remember feeling particularly pretty or unattractive. To be clean and well-groomed, I was told, was what was important.

As a young girl, I grew up in the projects of Hamilton, Ohio, which is located 20 miles north of Cincinnati. When I was in middle school, my mother and step-father moved us to a small home in a quiet neighborhood in Hamilton.

Unfortunately, there was constant discord in our home. My mother was a Christian, while my stepfather was not. The conflict and sometimes abusive behavior against my mother caused a lot of unrest.

I am the eldest of 11 children. My mother's first three children were from her first marriage. For this reason, I felt responsible for helping my mother maintain order domestically—and even emotionally. Although this should have been a time to feel care-free, instead, I was often burdened with concerns that I should not have had to carry.

When I completed 9th grade, my mother became concerned for the safety and welfare of my brother, sister and I—her three eldest children. For this reason, she made arrangements for us to live with her mother in West Virginia.

We arrived in time for me to enroll in my first year of High School. We lived in Logan County, snuggled in the mountains of a small town called Man. We lived in Kistler, a coal mining community or hollow. A hollow is a crevice between several mountains. We were so deeply enclosed, the only way to see the sky was to look straight up.

The move to West Virginia from a small town in Ohio was a dramatic change. As a matter of fact, it was extremely traumatic and unsettling. But, my grandmother was loving, attentive and a prize-winning cook. Most of our neighbors were friendly; black, white and mixed. We had a friendly co-existence—borrowing sugar and salt from one another, but, the whites went to their church and the "colored folk" went to theirs. We went to integrated schools, but, somehow, "getting religion" did not allow for racial co-existence.

We had chickens to feed, clothes to hang on the line and homework after school. Life was busy with church and chores, so, we had very little idle time. We settled into "Mama's" peaceful home; exposed to a lot of discipline and twice as much love.

St. James Baptist, our family church was next door and we were there almost every time the doors opened. I had always gone to church since I could remember, but, the Baptist were different from the Pentecostals I grew up with. The deacons would stand outside after church and smoke cigars and cigarettes. This was when I learned that "being saved" meant different strokes for different folks.

As a seventh grader, I needed lots of answers. I wanted to know why life had become so confusing. My grandmother wasn't a talker. She usually worked 6 days a week as a domestic. I was pensive most of the time. My transistor radio became my best friend and American Bandstand with Dick Clarke my entertainment on Saturdays until grandma's driver would drop her off at the house. Then the dancing would stop and the channel was turned. There was no dancing in her house—or at least those were the rules she had set.

I noticed the girls on American Bandstand wore fancy dresses and cuddled with the fellas—something I didn't think of doing. After all, I didn't feel that attractive.

When I was in grade school, an accident in physical education class caused me to chip my front tooth. Because it didn't get repaired until I was a senior in high school, I was self-conscious and would try to hold my lips together when I smiled. Being "pretty" or cute was not in my frame of reference. I was in hiding both physically and emotionally. I felt awkward and unsure about myself and the world around me. I was in survival mode.

No one knew however, that I was actually gaining strength and had almost emerged from a deep dark place. Before leaving my home in Hamilton, I was anything but a well-adjusted adolescent. I was already experiencing signs of chronic stress. My self-esteem had almost hit rock bottom. The discord, and arguments had gotten so bad in our home that I found myself pulling out my hair and eating it. I would also eat notebook paper and tiny pieces of cloth torn from clean sheets in my mother's rag box.

No one really knew the depth of my issues. I was very secretive about my activities. I later learned that this childhood eating disorder is called pica and can be brought about by emotional stress. For this reason, moving had been good for me. In the new environment, I found the peace and support I needed to become reasonably healthy and whole. In my new home, I was determine to grow up and change my habits. Somehow, I began to work through a measure of the pain and difficulty I had once suffered.

When a young person is struggling on the inside with trauma and stress—there is very little beauty to be found. My heart and spirit was broken. As I indicated before, I was in survival mode—just trying to make it from one day to the next without a complete breakdown. Having a doting grand-mother, attending Sunday School, church and receiving love and attention from my church family was healing.

At this time in my life, I was one of those "diamonds in the rough" literary scholars often talk about. The beauty of a woman is like a precious diamond ring that one might admire on a bride's wedding day. Diamonds begin in the heart of the earth. Once they are properly mined and processed, they have incredible value.

Beauty too requires a process. It's not the shape of a woman's face or the color of her skin. Beauty begins to be cultivated and nurtured when a woman is awakened to the potential of her true value and worth. One thing was always apparent to me at this time in my life. My grandmother knew her value and worth. I watched her get dressed for church. She looked beautiful and smelled amazing. I never knew my great grandparents, however, I am sure that somehow through life's process, she had been taught to hold her head up with dignity. Whether she felt it or not, she always looked confident.

She was also a giver. To see her baking bread for widows and the elderly was to me a beautiful site. This humble, yet ever so strong woman of God is the one who first introduced me to what it meant to look like a royal and to feel like one too. Again, she was a day-maid; a domestic who washed and ironed clothes for the wealthy. Yet, her specialty perfumes and taste in dress announced to all within her realm of influence that she was some kind of woman. It was a mind thing. She exemplified one who had been made strong through an arduous process. She was a diamond in the rough.

"Beauty is the delicate balance of impeccable taste, blended with discriminating character. It radiates from the inside out. It must be cared for, nurtured and treasured. When you believe—it's yours for keeps. The opinions of others do not matter."
–Brenda Joyce Johnson

I want to emphasize here that my first concept of beauty did not come from someone telling me that I was cute, pretty or beautiful. I picked up the attributes of beauty by watching the behavior of those around me. For other women, I'm sure their concept of beauty became a reality in other ways.

My spiritual foundation taught me that loving God was an appealing and desirable trait. Our pastor, Elder Neal, would talk about "walking in the beauty of holiness." I would hear my mother sing, "Let us walk in the light, the beautiful light. Shines all around us by day and by night. Jesus the light of the world." Her melodious voice was always comforting. I would also hear her crying out in prayer before the Lord. I learned to do the same. Both my mother and grandmother taught me as a child concepts of beauty and values I would learn to appreciate for a life-time.

BUILDING STRONG FOUNDATIONS

A report I recently read states that teenagers in single-parent families and blended families (which was my case) are three times more likely to need psychological help within a given year. (Peter Hill "Recent Advances in

Selected Aspects of Adolescent Development" Journal of Child Psychology and Psychiatry 1993). What if the trauma experienced goes unnoticed? In our home, everyone—especially my mother—from day to day, she was living in survival mode. living in survival mode. Somehow, we survived without anyone having a total breakdown.

The move to West Virginia, though unsettling, was the break I needed from my rag box and a church that did not know how to minister to their youth. Something changed mentally when I moved. The change of location and environment had been good for me. Somehow a certain reality kicked in. I knew that I had to grow up and wear my big girl panties. I could no longer hold onto a victim's mentality. I knew I had to learn to become a woman.

My grandmother had a good friend, Ms. Pennick. She was her Avon perfume lady who regularly visited to keep her supplied with fragrances and lotions. She was always exquisitely dressed. My grandmother also dressed to the nines. This mountain hillbilly-woman had class. Although she was a day maid and housekeeper during the week, she found her way to Copy Kat Boutique in downtown Man, West Virginia to shop for herself, my sister and me on the weekends. She bought our clothes from the same boutique where the ladies she worked for shopped. My sister, Phyllis, and I never got to shop from the main store. She would bring our dresses, skirts and blouses home with a variety of choices. We would choose a couple outfits at a time and the rest would go back to the store.

When I was around 10 years old, I accepted Jesus as Lord. I learned the beatitudes, ten commandments and about the faith of women in the Bible. I was taught that God is timeless and that my faith would open doors and move obstacles out of the way. Now that I was in High School, I knew I had to grow up and begin to "pretty up." I watched my girlfriends put on lipstick and then I began to wear bras and hose. I was beginning to feel stronger, different and special about myself. Most importantly, because from childhood I had been taught to love God, deep within, I knew I could trust Him.

Ecclesiastes 12:1 (paraphrased):
Remember your Creator in the days of your youth; while the evil days
come not ...before old age draws near when we will no longer take
pleasure in the physical things of life and have no enjoyment in them.

God is all-wise and knowing. Had my siblings and I not gotten the attention we needed—when we needed it, we could have been another statistic. Being the product of a broken home can have a devastating impact on one's life and impact the way we feel about ourselves. This was my truth. I recently read that seventy percent of long-term prison inmates grew up in broken homes. (Horn, Bush, "Fathers, Marriage and Welfare Reform.")

Although I was never a law-breaker or found myself incarcerated, it is chilling to look at these statistics and think this could have been my plight. My mother never wanted her marriage to end in divorce, however, like many women today, her circumstances left her feeling helpless. I don't think we know enough about the impact of growing up in an unstable home or the impact of divorce.

Ecclesiastes Verse 12:13 & 14:
Hear the conclusion (end) of the matter (life in general): Fear God, and
keep his commandments, for this is the whole duty of man. For God
shall bring every work into judgement, with every secret thing, whether
it be good or whether it be evil.

Having fear, which means reverence for God is the sum of what kingdom people are to be about. This is an amazing and conclusive verse! The Amplified version says, "Fear God—know that He is, revere and worship Him—and keep His commandments; for this is the whole duty of man (the full original purpose of his creation, the object of God's providence, the root of character, the foundation of all happiness, *the adjustment to all inharmonious circumstances and conditions* under the sun...).

Of course, this places a monumental responsibility on parents and caregivers. Proverbs 22:6 instructs parents to train up (dedicate and give instruction to) children in the way they should go; so that when they are old, they will not depart from it. (Proverbs 22:6). This scripture, ladies, indicates a lifetime journey.

From birth, God gives us a name and identity by way of our parents. I named my eldest Melissa Dawn. Melissa means "sweet—honey bee" and Dawn means "new day." Our second daughter's name is Angela Renee. Angela means "messenger of the Lord" and Renee' means "renaissance" or "rebirth." What we name our children is important. This is one way to give them significance and places a demand on their lives to live up to their "calling."

God has a desire to call us forth in honor and beauty. The role of parents should not be underestimated. Parents, when they step into their God-given responsibilities, provide identity markers to get us started in the right direction. Godly parents will ask the heavenly father for counsel and guidance regarding their child's future and direction. This will enable them to command a blessing over their children in a powerful way.

Perhaps your parents missed out on their privilege to partner with God in naming you—to affirm your "calling" and direction. As long as we are breathing, it's never too late to step into a role to mentor and or be a role model. Once we become knowledgeable about what is expected of us—we can ask forgiveness, if necessary, and submit our will to his.

BUILDING A SPIRITUAL FOUNDATION

As we delve more deeply into the topic of beauty, we must remember that our lives have spiritual roots. We mentioned already, it was Adam and

Eve's failure to listen and obey God's voice that ultimately caused calamity. Unfortunately, the mold was cast. What we see and hear can easily draw us away from the voice of God.

Since early 2020, globally, the world has been facing a major pandemic. Because of lockdowns and quarantines, more than ever, both young girls and women alike are engaged in online communications. Consequently, they are being influenced by images on social media.

"True Girl," (formerly Secret Keeper Girl) reports that 42% of church-going girls aged 12 and under report having smart phones with full access to the Internet. YouTube, Instagram and Snapchat are the most popular platforms. According to the Pew Research Center on Internet & technology, studies show that 95% of teens have access to smart phones and 45% report they are online almost constantly. For this reason, social media has a high stake in teen values and self-esteem.

For more than 11 years, the Dove soap brand has been an international leader in research to help women and girls build a healthy self-esteem. They claim to have reached 60 million young people in self-esteem education. In an online article written in May of 2020, Positive Body Confidence: How Social Media Can Affect Body Image, the following statement is made. "…the idea of 'checking in' online or sharing a selfie to let people know where you are and what you're up to might have seemed bizarre in the past, but, not today."

As we all know, for today's youth, teens and adults, getting "likes" on photos, posts, or comments in the virtual world brings personal satisfaction and a powerful sense of community acceptance. The article also states that, "While social media is not the cause of low self-esteem, it has all the right elements to contribute to it." Girls and women alike often get their "beauty fix" from social media messaging.

Social media has often become parent, moral guide and spiritual advisor. Media posts, comments and messages have been consequential in breaking up marriages and even resulted in suicide. Comments like, "Your hair looks great!" or "You've lost weight," can be considered the ultimate "get noticed" moment for those who are desperate for a compliment or a virtual hug. Unfortunately, women and girls alike, no matter the race or economic status are desperately lacking in their ability to see themselves as beautiful.

Here are more interesting statistical research findings by Dove: Only 4% of women around the world consider themselves beautiful (up from 2% in 2004). Only 11% of girls globally are comfortable describing themselves as "beautiful." Here's more:

- 72% of girls feel tremendous pressure to be beautiful

- 80% of women agree that every woman has something about her that is beautiful, but do not see their own beauty

- More than half of women globally (54% agree that when it comes to how they look, they are their own worst beauty critic.

The statistics outlined are clear indicators that the need for a woman to receive validation never changes—and continues to rise. We all need confidence boosters from time to time. Deep inside, most of us feel as if we are underperforming and inadequate in some form or fashion.

God has placed inside of each of us the desire to be attractive, accepted and "beautiful"—to get noticed for our attributes and accomplishments. None of us want to be rejected and ignored. From birth, our antennas are extended. We are seeking smiles, gestures and words of affirmation and acceptance.

I have taken the time to share some of the details of my unsettling beginnings, so that you will know some of the good, bad and ugly that began shaping my attitudes regarding life and what is beautiful. Some of the spiritual underpinnings were there; but, many were not. We may have all had different family lives and may have been born and reared in other circumstances or countries. We all, however, suffer from many of the same insecurities.

When I was growing up, I wasn't told I was cute, pretty or beautiful. Everyone around me seemed to be in survival mode. I carried a sad countenance and knew there was something missing. I simply didn't have the vocabulary or awareness as to what that something could be. Understanding what God had in mind for us in the beginning gives us a context for life.

BEAUTY IN THE KINGDOM

Studying and grasping the secrets of God's heart as revealed in scripture is life-changing. When I pull out my concordance to do word studies, I find nuggets of truth that began to illuminate my understanding. The word "beautiful" can be found in scripture in both positive and negative contexts. One of the dozens of scriptures where the word "beautiful" can be found is in Ecclesiastes 3:11. Here the word is defined as "good and pleasant."

This passage tells us that God has made everything *beautiful* in its time. This is most educational and instructive—alluding to a required process. Process implies "a procedure or method requiring a course of action." Interestingly enough, because I've studied manners and etiquette, I understand that this whole field requires a learning process of managing behavior. A thoughtful process of consideration, care and concern for others is required, to build healthy relationships.

In biblical word studies, the term beautiful not only means good, honorable, pleasant and pleasing—but also reminds us that all that God made was good. In my research, I was also introduced to the connection between the word "beautiful" and the "kingdom of heaven."

Of course, the word kingdom means the reign and dominion of a king. We also know that a king must be honored. He represents our highest ideals of that which is to be respected. God is sovereign over all the earth. His kingdom is worthy of all glory and honor. Matthew 13:45 tells us that all that we can desire can be found within the kingdom:

…the kingdom of heaven is like unto a merchant man seeking goodly (beautiful) pearls. Who, when he found one pearl of great price, went and *sold all that he had*, and bought it.

As I understand this parable, the man came seeking what he considered to be of great value; but, found much more—something priceless.

The disciples, who were the followers of Jesus asked him: "Why do you speak to us in parables?" Jesus answered them saying: "These are truths; hidden mysteries passed down from generation to generation from your fathers." (Psalm 78:2). The scriptures also explains that parables would only be understood by those who had been converted or initiated into the mysteries of the kingdom.

The truth to be revealed from Matthew 13:45 was to make known to his disciples the value and worth of having possession and ownership to the valuables of the kingdom. To seek such beauty and to find it is worth everything!

Another truth revealed as I studied the word beautiful from scripture came from Mark 9:50, which speaks of salt as good (beautiful, pleasing). But, if the salt have lost *his* saltiness, why use it for seasoning? It is good for nothing. Then the scripture admonishes us to ***Have salt (beauty) in yourselves***, and have peace one with another.

How powerful and life-transforming to know this truth. The heart of God is that we would have beauty within. Pearls have a charming appeal, having been painstakingly processed by nature so that they are exquisitely beautiful and highly desirable. But, to know that God made the ultimate beauty available by way of his kingdom is a priceless truth. These are the mysteries God wants to convey to us today—truths only apparent to his initiated ones.

For this reason, God sent his son who paid the ultimate price for us—he sacrificed the life of his only son so that we might live. To our Father God, we were worth it. However, if we have no perception of our beauty, we are like tasteless salt with no value or purpose. Although we have been endued with power from on high, we become weak and useless to the kingdom.

To find favor with God by confessing our faults and accepting Jesus Christ as Lord is the pathway to the beauty and riches of the kingdom. To have this pearl of great price is worth giving up all that we have accumulated and accomplished in exchange for this treasure. Romans 10:9 & 10 gives us keys to the wealth of the kingdom:

That if you shall confess with your mouth the Lord Jesus, and shall believe in your heart that God raised him from the dead, you shall be saved.

Once we accept Jesus Christ as Lord, the beauty of salvation and the gift of the holy spirit comes to live inside of us. This is actually the heart of the *beauty mystique.* From the beginning of time, God's dream was that his nature would be deposited in us when we believe. The fullness of this mystery was made known on the day of Pentecost.

Colossians 1:27 tells us that God wanted to make known the glorious wealth of this hidden mystery for ages and generations. Finally, he has revealed it to us...*which is Christ in you the hope of glory*. Ephesians 1:12 says that he gave us this gift so that our lives would be to the praise of his glory.

So, as believers, we can relax. We no longer need to feel deprived and deficient. The "beauty mystique" is not a shallow concept revealing the intricacies of some unattainable goal. It is not some complicated formula describing how to become more physically attractive. It does not consist of contemporary notions shaped by social media and Netflix. It does not begin with coloring our hair or making a stunning fashion statement.

Make-up, physical charm and beauty alone, will not change how people who need a transformational "touch from God" view us. Our spirituality and ability to submit to the plan of God is the only thing that will draw those whom he loves and wants to bring into his kingdom. He desires to place his spirit inside so they can be transformed from the inside out.

Women are nurturers by nature. God uses our natural and spiritual gifts to supernaturally draw individuals out of themselves. We beckon them to come close, so they can get the fullness of what God has. As we listen, speak and observe—we become sensitive to his voice. He speaks to us and there is a tri-fold exchange. We listen and share what he is saying to us and in return, all are blessed. This supernatural exchange is the workings of the *beauty mystique* live and in color. God is present and in the mix—ministering and nurturing our generation and culture to health.

This is what causes us to be "different" as women of God. Our influence is not natural, but, supernatural. Having a life submitted to Christ means we are no longer living selfishly—enslaved to selfish desires—thinking only of pleasing ourselves. Instead, we have been transformed; liberated to live free from the bondage of our sinful flesh.

This freedom allows our new nature—the beauty of the Christ in us to manifest itself so that his nature comes alive in us and through us. Our transformational life-style can be summed up in Galatians 5:14: The *entire* law (custom by which we live) is summed up in a single command: "Love your neighbor as yourself." What a beautiful manifesto of life! A declaration of what the scriptures mean when it states, "thy kingdom come, thy will be done, in earth as it is in heaven."

THE WOMAN SCORNED

So, since the manifest "glory" of God has been deposited in the earth and in us, why are we as women subject to and imprisoned by childlike guilt? Why are we being tormented and plagued by our shortcomings—trying to live by the expectations of others? Why do we allow ourselves to be burdened by the allurements of Vanity Fair and O' Magazine and feel inadequate if we do not measure up?

The truth is that there is a sinister force lurking beneath the images we see and voices we hear. Just like Eve, we are often blind sighted by enticements that lure us away, causing us to question and doubt God's word. The influences are subtle. They too are beautiful and attractive—but, only to the eye of the uninitiated ones.

This counterfeit spirit seeks to undermine God's dream. From the beginning of time, God's arch enemy, Satan, has sought to diminish and disrupt the power of God in the earth. He has an explicit distaste for the woman.

The book of revelation reveals this age-old vendetta Satan has had with God from the beginning of time. Front and center in this drama is the woman—the life-spring of humanity—the mother of all living.

In Revelation 12:3-12, we find God's arch enemy, Satan, who is described as "a great red dragon." This very real threat to her very existence is prophetically described by "John the revelator," as it plays out in the realm of the spirit. The "drama" begins with a glimpse of the insurrection of God's most beautiful and talented of his created beings. Because of pride and rebellion, not only was Satan, but, one third of the angelic beings were cast down to earth.

In this passage, we find Satan's plan to undermine God's purposes being manifested. He seeks to devour Jesus as soon as he is born. Let's follow this drama as it unfolds.

Vs. 3: And there appeared another wonder in heaven; and behold a great red dragon, having seven heads and ten horns, and seven crowns upon his heads.

Vs 4: And his tail drew the third part of the stars of heaven and did cast them to the earth: and the dragon stood before the woman which was ready to be delivered, for to devour her child as soon as it was born.
Vs. 5: And she (Mary) brought forth a man child (Jesus) who was to rule all nations with a rod of iron: and her child was caught up unto God (the resurrection), and to his throne.

Vs. 6: And the woman fled into the wilderness, where she hath a place prepared of God...

Vs. 7: And there was war in heaven: Michael and his angels fought against the dragon; and the dragon fought and his angels,

Vs. 8: and prevailed not; neither was their place found any more in heaven.

Vs. 9: And the great dragon was cast out, that old serpent, called the Devil, and Satan which deceives the whole world: and he was cast down into the earth, and his angels were cast out with him...

Vs. 10: And I heard a loud voice saying in heaven, Now is come salvation, and strength, and the kingdom of our God, and the power of his Christ: for the accuser of our brethren is cast down, **which accused them before our God day and night.**

Vs 11: And they (God's people) overcame him by the blood of the Lamb, and by the word of their testimony; and they loved not their lives unto the death.

Vs 12: Therefore rejoice, ye heavens, and he that dwell in them. Woe to those who inhabit the earth and of the sea! For the devil is come down unto you, having great wrath, because he knows that he hath (only) a short time.

Next, let's look at Revelation 12:17, which is a key scripture that will help you, as a woman of God, understand the warfare and the battle that began with Eve and is yet playing out on the stage of time. This warfare is not only against women, *but the woman's (God's) precious seed.*

Vs. 17 (Amplified version): So then the dragon was furious (enraged) at the woman, and he went away to wage war on the remainder of her descendants who obey God's commandments and who have the testimony of Jesus Christ—and adhere to it and bear witness to Him.

So, here we are today. Take heart woman of God! Welcome to an ongoing saga—same stage—same theme—different scene. The chaos continues. Is it no wonder that many of us have struggled a lifetime—first with one issue—and then another. We are not imagining things! The warfare is real. Some of us are seeing or facing broken engagements and marriages, loneliness, barrenness, suicide, infanticide, breast cancer, gender confusion, abortion, heart disease and more. All have a sinister root cause. But, thank God for Jesus. He can heal, forgive and set us free.

Could it be that much of what we suffer can be traced back to our femininity? Yes, of course, Satan does not like or favor our counterpart, men either. However, there is a specific loathe he carries for you—and your seed. From you springs life! When you accepted Jesus as your Lord, you partnered with God to bring forth God's seed—both in the natural and in the spirit.

More than ever, we see a cultural war going on. The world may call it political. I call it spiritual. Never before in my life-time have I seen such anti-American and anti-Christian rhetoric. God has made you, his "word-enforcement officer." Don't back down and don't give up on being "biblically correct". There is no such thing as being "politically correct," because within all parties there are diversified ideologies and opinions.

You are a wellspring of life gushing forth –nurturing and refreshing. You have been called and chosen to partner with your heavenly Father as the mother of all living. Maybe you were not blessed to birth a child, however, *You*, oh woman of God have dynamic and destiny written all over you. Walk in it. It's time for you to join the Ruth's, Esther's and Anna's in biblical history. It's time for you to get noticed!

THE PRACTICAL SIDE OF BEAUTY

A self-assured and confident woman of God walks with majesty and power both in the natural and in the spirit. Her smile is inviting and her manner is considerate and kind. Even when she is perplexed, she knows how to take a deep breath and ascend into prayer.

When she enters a room, she can take her place without causing a fuss. Her demeanor will quietly announce that she has arrived. Her warm and inviting presence shows that she is poised, prepared and ready to get the job done. Maya Angelou speaks of the power of presence in this way:

"When you know you are of worth – not asking it, but knowing it, you walk into a room with a particular power.

When you know you are of worth, you don't have to raise your voice, you don't have to become rude, you don't have to become vulgar; you just are.

And you are like the sky is, as the air is, the same way water is wet. It doesn't have to protest – it just is."
–Maya Angelou

Dr. Angelou calls this unique quality a "particular power." Many of us have heard the phrase, "Knowledge is power." When we know more, we can practice more, and do more with the qualities we possess. Women who know the power and influence of "presence," bring an empowering message to everything they do. The job gets done without a noisy show. I'm sometimes amused by women who project power by taking lessons to deepen their voice. They shop for a "power look" to appear more masculine. To top it off, they throw around expletives to show that they are in charge.

One of a woman's greatest assets is her ability to be influential rather than abrasive. She can literally change the atmosphere of almost any situation simply by being a good listener. Taking the time to give people the attention they deserve builds credibility and respect. A great place to begin showing your power as a woman is to embrace the uniqueness of your feminine qualities. The significance of your voice comes chiming through, simply because you're you!

MY TRANSFORMATION JOURNEY

I'm a graduate of Roland's International School of Modeling in Fayetteville, North Carolina. One of the goals and objectives of a modeling school is to teach students how to look and feel confident and attractive. At first, I felt intimidated and out of place. No one enrolled in the class was like me.

Although I was fearful and unsure of what I would experience, I enrolled anyway. I did it not only to build my self-esteem, but to improve myself for the sake of my daughters. After all, how could I give them what I lacked myself?

I also saw a great need in our community to help young girls who needed affirmation and encouragement. It was obvious to me that they needed answers regarding femininity, as well as how they fit into this complicated puzzle called life.

Without a doubt, I made the right choice. My inquiring mind and desire to learn, allowed me to experience the journey of a lifetime. I quickly learned that the pursuit would be challenging, however, I was committed and resolute in pursuing the process to a successful finish.

All of my classmates were White and all but one was in their teens and early 20's except for one lady who was a television anchor. She enrolled to polish her media presence. I was in my mid-30s.

Enrolling in modeling school was one of my first steps to designing the person I wanted to become. As I eagerly settled into my classes, I learned to become more poised and confident. Although I experienced moments of apprehension, I met the challenge and won a trophy in our graduation competition.

The journey solidified a strong foundation that equipped me to go first-class all the way. I kicked aside the excuses that made me feel inadequate and turned them into reasons for conquering the dragon of doubt and fear that clung to my personae since childhood. I registered for workshops, excursions, fashion shows and conferences to learn techniques and to observe professionals in the field. They were my mentors. My confidence grew with every experience.

I believe this is a great time to share some keys to looking fabulous wherever you go. There are "insider secrets" used by professionals who not only command the stage when they are on stage, but, no matter where they go, people take notice.

ELEMENTS OF PRESENCE

Although we are fascinated, and sometimes even suspect of the designer themes we see gracing the haute de' couture runway, we should take note of their perfect posture. Haute couture means a garment that is top-level and hand customized, by or for an exclusive fashion design house. Before the lights come on and the show begins, countless hours have gone into practice and preparation.

In modeling school, we were taught that models are the coat hangers for the clothes we love. They cannot afford to slump their shoulders or walk with their heads down. Their carriage makes a definitive statement, while making the garment come to life.

We were also taught that, "Beauty is an illusion." This was a liberating concept for me, because I really needed to know how to appreciate my unique full lips and brown skin. I knew I was created in the image and likeness of God. I was not beautiful because I look like others, but, because I was created with a uniqueness that was my very own. I had to, however, begin to not only like, but, to love me—everything about the physical part of me that I could not change.

To project confidence, one must feel confident. Posture is foundational to perfect presence. Standing and sitting straight and tall projects a self-assured personae and is one of the first principles of creating a positive self-image. Posture is important for the following reasons:

- It gives the appearance of confidence and poise.

- It aligns the body for a more youthful appearance.

- It allows inner organs to function properly.

- It helps clothing fit and hang better on the body-frame.

I am convinced that behind every positive first-impression is not only a smile, but squared shoulders standing or sitting erect and ready to take on any challenge.

MASTERING THE ART OF SITTING, WALKING & STANDING

The disciplines of learning to sit, walk and stand with impressive body posture are all elements of non-verbal communication.

- To check your posture, place your heels against a flat-wall; stand erect in front of a mirror, stomach tucked-in, shoulders pulled-back and legs close together.

- Remember—perfect posture will add more to the distinction of your appearance than most anything else.

- To sit, don't fall in the chair. Reach for the forward edge or sides of the seat. Use leg muscles to slide gently into the seat.

- Sit tall—use the same technique to rise. Slide forward, allowing your weight to be over your feet—then rise.

- Walk with energy and purpose being careful not drag your feet.

- Do not lean on furniture, podiums, desks, tables or the wall.

- When standing, keep your hands out of your pockets and don't jingle change or keys.

OUR FACIAL EXPRESSIONS & GESTURES

- Learn to manage your expressions, no matter how you are feeling. Frowns and sneers communicate a bad attitude.

- Hand gestures send important ques—don't point when you speak. Instead, open your hands with your palms-up, to communicate your point of view which indicates you are open to receive.

- Don't tap on a table or desk or keep checking your cell phone or watch during conversations. This gesture can communicate irritability and impatience.

- Keep your hands away from your hair. Flipping or combing your hair in public is inappropriate.

- When sitting at a table, keep your hands visible.

- It's rarely acceptable to whisper in the company of others. Ask for a private conversation away from the group.

Training as a model was the perfect foundation for me to build self-awareness. I learned that poise, personality and appearance are the three key components for positive stage presence—and for making a positive first impression.

Poise—The ability to carry oneself with grace, self-assurance and grace.

Personality—A congenial, kind and cordial manner. This can be shown and expressed in a vibrant and spirited movement and walk.

Appearance—Intentional time and effort is invested in presenting a stunning and immaculate presence using creativity in wardrobe, color, style, hair and make-up.

Standing up and out is not only important for those who walk the runway, but for each of us. We all have a significant role to play in culture and society. Our ability to carry a compelling presence becomes evident when we understand our greater goal which is to represent the king of glory who made and created us for His glory.

Matthew 5:14 (NIV): "You are the light of the world. A city on a hill cannot be hidden. Do people light a lamp and put it under a bowl? Instead they put it on its stand and it gives light to everyone... In the same way, let your light shine before men, that they may see your good deeds and praise your Father in heaven."

We are God's masterpiece—made in his image to reflect his majesty and glory. How we do this is limited only to the degree that we acknowledge and understand our spiritual heritage.

SILENT MESSAGES

Another intriguing concept regarding the *beauty mystique* is the significance of silent messaging. We've heard it said time-and-again: "We never get a second chance to make a first impression." My mantra to you is... "Silently, we speak the loudest."

That's because, before we speak, most individuals observing us have already made a judgement regarding our education, intelligence, economic status, and whether or not they want to know us.

Have you ever watched people at the mall? We may not be aware, but we evaluate another person's appearance and draw conclusions that she or he must be a business person, a stay-at-home-mom, a silly teenager, or a college student. Many of us would rather think we're not guilty of prejudging, but this is simply human nature. We see what we see, and come to a logical, or even an illogical conclusion. We tend to mentally categorize others, placing them into easily sortable groups.

That's the foundational definition for the word "prejudice." In essence it means to judge prematurely before we have all the facts. We all do it—both consciously and subconsciously. Sometimes we miss the mark by putting individuals in categories they don't belong—because of the color of their skin, political persuasion, or because they drive a luxury car. We prematurely decide they are not worthy of our attention.

Our facial expressions, posture, gestures and clothing, speak volumes without us saying a word. This can also be unfair. Often, we make business and social decisions about others without taking time for a conversation. As a result, we make hasty judgments that may or may not be true.

In business endeavors, image educators call this category of training and development "soft skills." We work with individuals to help them improve their body language, tone of voice and gestures so that they can intentionally work to create the right impressions. We all, however, must manage our thinking—trying to always be our best, and believe the best about others.

BODY LANGUAGE

Here are some checkpoints to evaluate your body language...

- Do you point and move your hands rhythmically as you speak and articulate a thought?

- Do you shrug your shoulders to show disinterest or begin to look anxiously away when you don't want to talk?

- Do you communicate your anxiety by clicking your pen or tampering with your bracelet?

- Do you keep your hands in your pocket, standing aloof and non-engaged while conversing with others?

- Do you squint and frown when you have difficulty with an unfamiliar accent or disagree with someone?

- Do you peer over the top rim of your glasses? This can appear condescending or create the impression that you are not believed.

If you answered yes to any of these questions, you may want to pay attention to your non-verbal signals. Remember that first impressions always count. The perception received by the person observing your actions is their reality. Non-verbal language is always speaking before we say a word.

ELEMENTS OF COMMUNICATION

A personal communications expert, Professor Albert Mehrabian of UCLA, conducted a study to measure verbal, vocal and visual elements of communication. According to his research, when there are inconsistencies in the way we communicate, it impacts our believability rating. There are three elements of communication:

55% Appearance (posture, facial expressions, gestures, grooming and dress)

38% Voice (tone and inflections)

7% Words (how thoughts are articulated)

Experts in the field of image and etiquette use this formula to illustrate the significance and importance of non-verbal communication skills. Until I was trained to advise others to become better communicators in these areas, I had no concept or understanding of how one category could supersede the other. The fact remains that before an initial introduction, individuals formulate opinions regarding others—deciding whether they are interested in engaging in conversation or business *within the first 30-to-60 seconds.*

The deciding factor is predominantly what they see and observe—or appearance. For this reason, my mantra to you remains, "Silently, we speak the loudest."

This information may surprise you, as we've always been told to watch what we say. However, we must remember the significance of appearance. We know good grooming and being polite is important, but did you know that your facial expression, gestures and posture are also in the appearance category?

The truth is this... no matter what you say, you aren't believable until your appearance and non-verbal messages line-up with your speech. Attractiveness is not simply how well you apply your make-up to mirror the ladies in fashion magazines. On the contrary, being attractive and beautiful as we've already discussed, is an intricate balance of impeccable grooming, excellence in manners and dress; with the spirit and heart of Christ shining through.

Remember that there is an invisible and sometimes not so invisible audience awaiting your arrival. They are anxious to rate your worthiness for the next promotion, or there may be a potential life partner observing you. Choose not to disappoint, but be prepared and ready to excel and succeed on the stage called life. The way we are perceived can either be a gateway to an exceptional future, or a deep dive into obscurity. It's your choice.

TAKING A FINAL LOOK

A lot of truth can be found about personal beauty by taking an honest look in the mirror. Ask yourself two questions: "What kind of compliments do I get?" and "What kind of compliments would I like to get?" Then begin to make mental notes. This is where the "Change Formula" from the previous chapter comes to life. You'll never create a vision for change, unless you become dissatisfied with the status quo and take action. We must be ok with becoming uncomfortable in our comfort zones.

One thing is for sure, we take the worst and the best of ourselves everywhere we go. We must learn to acknowledge, with truth and honesty, what makes us feel insecure and find solutions to deal with feelings of inadequacy. It's always good to stop, look, listen and self-evaluate. This process challenges us and reveals negative thoughts that must be replaced with positive ones. Although I desperately desired to improve my appearance and manners, I lacked the knowledge to excel in these critical areas of life.

Once I was honest and stopped telling myself, "Well, that's just the way I am," I could move forward and face reality. I had learned to hide behind excuses. But, trying to hide my inadequacies left me feeling even more insecure. Modeling school helped me address areas in my personality and appearance that made me uncomfortable. I learned that change required me to accept gut-wrenching truths about my posture, hair, skin, voice and wardrobe. It took courage and introspection to face unsettling and unpleasant realities.

We can only learn to reverse these insecurities when we begin to identify what is plaguing us! One liberating truth I learned in modeling school was, "It is ok to be different." I challenge you to give yourself permission to be different! Your nose, hair, size of your feet and color of your skin can all work to your advantage, if you will accept who you are, and what you are as beautiful. This is not about someone else's opinion. This is about you! Give yourself permission to be different!

Perhaps you're a college student who is aspiring to become a professional. Maybe you're a retired person wanting to start a business. Whatever your station in life, now is the time to get a fresh perspective and upgrade. Ask yourself:

- "Am I happy with my looks and appearance?"

- "What appeals to me and what does not?"

- "What must I do to bring about change?"

Beauty, in its simplicity, simply means to have balance and uniformity. When we are out of balance, we feel unapproachable, unappreciated, and unattractive. When we feel balanced, we radiate with presence and attract those around us. People want to come close—to take another look. Once you ask these questions and begin to work on areas that you are not comfortable with, you will see transformation taking place right before your eyes.

As Shania Twain says, you are the mother of the human race. Mother means "source" and "origin." We have the talent and potential to transcend the limitations set by others. Take a peek into the essence of your own soul. Ask God in prayer these two questions: "Who am I?" and "How can I be all that you created me to be?"

When we inquire—seeking God's guidance, we receive the answers we need as did Thomas in John 14:6-7. Here we find Jesus speaking to Thomas who wanted to know how he could find the way of life. Thomas, was of course, speaking of the way of the life in the spirit.

Jesus answered and said, "I am the way and the truth and the life. No one comes to the Father except through me. If you really knew me, you would know my Father as well." The discipline required to learn the life of the spirit is a journey that we must all find. Whether male or female, this is the core of our existence. Without a core, there's no seed and consequently, no holy spirit to produce the needed virtues of life. The spirit is the true essence of all that is beautiful in and about our lives.

The word of God provides the master beauty plan. The mystery that was hid before the foundations of the earth is written in this plan—which is "Christ in you—the hope of glory." If Satan had known that by causing the death of the Lord of glory, he would enable the release of armies of warrior women like us—I don't think he would have orchestrated his vicious plot.

Nevertheless, by God's Providence and grace, we have been empowered with beauty and majesty of the great "I Am." Allow the following scriptures to encourage and affirm you daily.

I AM
I am called of God — Timothy 1:9
I am chosen – I Thessalonians 1:4
I am the apple of my Father's eye – Psalm 17:8
I am being changed into His image – II Corinthians 3:18
I am a new creation – II Corinthians 5:17
I am the temple of the Holy Spirit – I Corinthians 6:19
I am forgiven of all my sins – Ephesians 1:7
I am redeemed from the curse of the law – Galatians 3:9
I am blessed – Galatians 3:9
I am above and not beneath – Deuteronomy 28:13
I am His elect – Colossians 3:12
I am victorious – Revelations 12:11
I am fearfully and wonderfully made – Psalm 139:14

No matter who you are or where you live—there is nothing to compare with the effulgence and radiance of the beauty that glows from within your life once the Holy Spirit makes His deposit in your soul. Your beauty is born of the radiance that is in Christ Jesus. So shine, kingdom woman shine. Be your own kind of beautiful!

CHAPTER THREE

PERSONALITY PUZZLERS

THERE IS NOTHING ordinary about you! Perhaps you are complex at times; sometimes difficult to understand and seemingly always changing. Fascinating how people can misunderstand our objectives and intentions. Sometimes they are suspect and other times accepting. If we pause too long to figure it all out, we won't get much else done.

This phenomenon is one of my favorite topics because it has always stumped me. Why? Because I am the one who always wanted to be accepted. After all, I'm such a nice person. I wouldn't harm a flea. I would sometimes ask myself, "Why do you get the cold shoulder look so often?" You know—the "What are you grinning about?" look or response.

When we are "nice," some people think we must "want" something. Others think you must be asking for special favors. Who knows what people are thinking! This I do know—behind every set of eyes is a perspective that is often different from yours. Period. I've learned that I am not the judge or justifier of other's opinions. I have only one responsibility. That is to be true to my own values and convictions.

Personality traits are indeed complicated, mystical and many times are hard to figure out. However, to some degree, the mystery can be evaluated and interpreted according to "the rules" of the game established by those who study interpersonal relationships.

In order to be our confident best, we must take a look at how to understand people and their multi-faceted personality traits. We want to know how certain behaviors, preferences and "people styles" impact and impede self-confidence and likeability.

It's no secret that a person's personality can be an image maker or breaker. Our goal is to take another step in understanding who we are as individuals. We want to know why we accept and gravitate toward certain personality types and why we reject others.

Have you discovered that family members and those in close relationship with you can be your strongest critics? I experienced this growing up, which caused me to feel like an oddity. I discovered that harsh criticism of my body shape was injurious to me. I was not the kind of kid or young adult that could simply laugh off a snide remark. I had the kind of personality that would take a negative comment and dwell upon it rather than simply dismissing it and letting it go.

Personality traits are innate. We're all born with certain proclivities. Just watch small children, siblings who are raised in the same environment but whose personalities are completely different and often clash. You'll see as you progress in this chapter that our preferences simply reveal our true nature as human beings—whether we enjoy solitude or prefer being the life of the party is neither good nor bad. It's just our inner nature coming forth.

If only I'd known this early in life! That's why I'm so passionate about this chapter. I know the pain and agony that can be experienced when we don't know our truth. I had finished college and was well into my adult life when I discovered that I wasn't a shy lackluster person. I also began to understand that it was okay to be playful, talkative and extremely sensitive… all at the same time. That it wasn't an oddity… It was simply the complexities of me.

Feeling good in your own skin is a journey of self-discovery. It requires that we politely refute and reject the opinions of those who impose their likes and dislikes on us. Despite what critics might think or say, we are simply expressing what's normal for us. Our best defense is being ourselves.

Many people succeed when others do not believe in them. But rarely does a person succeed when he does not believe in himself.
–Herb True

Shall I repeat this truth for emphasis? Do you feel like you're cramped and all squished in a box; bound to the way your mom, uncle or husband says you need to be? They may say "You need to stop being so touchy feely—keep your opinions to yourself." Perhaps they are right. Maybe you do need to tone it down a bit, but don't allow anyone to make you feel inferior.

I've consulted and advised women who shop at the best boutiques, wear designer jeans and expensive perfumes, yet their self-image is broken because they never learned to deal with their inner-fear of not feeling accepted.

I remember a lady who came to me in tears after she completed my workshop. During the session, she realized the reason she wore big bangs with a lot of hair in her face, and large rimmed glasses was to hide her face because she felt ugly. She never knew she was hiding! She finally admitted that she didn't know how to be herself or let her true personality come forth. Unknowingly, she had begun to hide—behind her hair and glasses.

It takes courage to deal with our weaknesses and feelings of insecurity because we really don't know what we will uncover when the layers are peeled back. But this is the price of experiencing true freedom. I believe the bars of imprisonment that incarcerate the mind can be far more debilitating than the walls of a physical prison. Although I have never been in a real jail, I know men and women who have been; some wrote their very first book or penned their first poem while there and soared beyond the walls of their confinement. Freedom of expression is priceless.

Even while free in the physical sense, dark thoughts and oppressive feelings become "image barriers" because they impede your freedom of expression and keep you from building healthy relationships. Once you're aware of those debilitating thoughts, you can turn them into positive affirmations that allow you to crush old habits while forming new ones.

ACCEPTING YOUR PERSONALITY GIFT PACKAGE

Our personalities are at the core of who we are. Women who desire to present their best don't want to be misunderstood or offensive. Instead, they simply want freedom of expression. For me, this meant simply accepting and embracing my "personality gift package." I knew, however, my challenge would be controlling my tendency to be talkative and playful without shutting other people down.

Accepting one's personality as a gift is a good place to build wholesome and satisfying relationships. It's no fun to be mislabeled as I was during my childhood. It was liberating to know the truth about personality differences and to discover that I wasn't odd after all... just different.

Let's examine in more detail what some might call the complexities of the personality puzzle. You may discover some intriguing facts about who you really are—or have the potential to become.

This is a good place to make a distinction between the two words "temperament" and "personality," which some think are synonymous. Your temperament is what you are born with. Your personality is how you express this "gift."

Psychologists, therapists, life coaches and human resource business professionals identify two innate characteristics of human nature that are the underpinnings of personality, and help determine the outcome. I'm sure you've heard the terms—extrovert and introvert.

Although, some of us tend to be a combination of the two, when we look closely, one trait will almost always dominate.

CHARACTERISTICS OF EXTROVERTS:

- A natural leader.

- Enjoys meeting and connecting with people.

- Has good verbal skills and finds conversation easy.

- Seeks verification, confirmation, affirmation from outside themselves.

- Enjoys entertaining, using artistic abilities to express innermost feelings.

- Energized when they're with others—the life of the party.

- Has a good sense of humor—the center of attention.

- Feels bored or drained from spending too much time alone.

- Figures things out by talking things over with others.

- Easy to get acquainted with (most often).

- Speaks first and thinks later (many occasions).

Strengths:

Often delightful, a promoter, daring, spirited, cheerful, popular, positive, decisive, friendly, resourceful, funny, optimistic, encouraging, artistic, creative, and demonstrative.

Weaknesses:

Can be: Talkative, brassy, forgetful, show-off, changeable, loud, bossy, nervy, naive, unpredictable, undisciplined, disorganized, restless, impulsive, edgy, and flamboyant.

CHARACTERISTICS OF INTROVERTS:

- Enjoys spending time alone to analyze and figure things out.

- Can find spending time with others draining; especially with strangers.

- Seeks verification, confirmation and affirmation from inside themselves.

- Holds back from sharing thoughts or opinions with people, and may get left out.

- Has good writing skills and may prefer sharing thoughts in writing.

- Generally difficult to get acquainted with.

- Have a hidden side that surprises people when they reveal what they are thinking.

- Tend to be good listeners and make good counselors and confidants.

- They can be suspicious, rather than trusting.

- Tend to be more aware of inner thoughts and reactions, verses outer environment.

Strengths:

Often scheduled, has a dry humor, detail oriented, listener, balanced, deep, cultured, orderly, peaceful, mediator, tolerant, planner, idealistic, persistent, faithful, consistent, and predictable.

Weaknesses:

Can be shy, doubtful, hesitant, resentful, moody, loner, suspicious, withdrawn, revengeful, critical, depressed, rigid, insecure, procrastinator, fearful, plain, sensitive, reticent, inflexible, and hard to please.

Identifying innate personality traits is important for you to become "comfortable in your skin." Ask yourself these questions—what category do you fall in and why?

HOW TO BRING BALANCE

It is simply not true that introverts don't enjoy laughing and having fun. Conversely, it is also true that extroverts can enjoy sitting quietly while reading a book. Both, however, have proclivities that dictate preferences. These characteristics are innate and can be seen in early childhood. With the application of growth and maturity, adjustments can be made to bring a balance that's pleasing and rewarding no matter where you fall on the scale.

So, no more wishing you could be an outgoing individual. No need to beat yourself up because of comments you've heard or behavior that offended you. If you enjoy reading and prefer being alone, there's value in your personality. You may become the scientist who develops a cure for cancer or, because of your "gift for gab" you may be the next Oprah. The point is, recognize who you are and what brings you joy and happiness. Celebrate your strengths and embrace the uniqueness of you. Work on your weaknesses—to bring balance to the whole.

UNDERSTANDING YOUR PERSONALITY TYPE

So, who's to say when it's okay to be outspoken, or to keep our comments to ourselves? Here's where we get stumped on the complexities of personality. Of course, each of us must determine where our freedoms and boundaries lie. God gave us what I call, "inside sensors" known as intuition, which serves us well when we need to decide when to turn it on or shut it down.

"Waiting for some people to stop talking is like looking for the end of a roller towel.
–Nuggets

Just in case you don't understand the old fashioned term "roller towel," it refers to a roll of towels... like the one that keeps rolling when it's dropped—it goes on and on. I bet someone you know just came to mind. Being silent for this person is a difficult chore.

Of course, we also knew at least one wallflower in high school. She had very little to say and was criticized for it. She would retreat to hold up the wall when she didn't want to be bothered.

Then, of course, there was "Letty Loud Mouth," who had an opinion about everything and always had a secret to tell. Everyone remembers her. When she was around, we made sure we kept our secrets to ourselves.

Once we reach adulthood, we become less tolerant of the "Letty's" in our lives and recognize the importance of thinking before we speak.

If you're a more reserved type, you would rather watch than participate. You're probably fed-up with people trying to drag or coax you onto the dance floor. You might give in, but not without giving them "the look." Let's take a closer look at extroverts and introverts and focus on how each can influence our social lives and business environments.

INTERPERSONAL RELATIONSHIPS
Extrovert/Personal Characteristics

The Director: This person wants to be in control and is either the leader or is known to take the lead. When interacting with this personality type, the Analyzer (sometimes called the "supporter") will be less impulsive, bringing a listening ear to the table. This person brings balance to the relationship when the Director type is in charge.

The Persuader: This is a "people person," who shows creativity and influence. They work well with Analyzers or Supporters who are listeners. Together, they can easily map out a plan to bring a project or initiative to completion.

Introvert/Personal Characteristics

The Supporter: This person has the ability to listen and be empathetic. They are good counselors. In a work environment, a Supporter provides balance to both the Director and Persuader.

The Analyzer: This person has a cautious nature and excels as a scientist or researcher. Because they are planners and schedulers, they can also slow down productivity. They bring balance to the Persuader or Director, who has the proclivity to get things done.

WHY CAN'T WE JUST GET ALONG?

Now that I've outlined the different personalities types and their characteristics, can you find your personality type and how you best interrelate with others? Think about your best friend or your spouse. In what ways are you alike? In what ways are you different? Does your personality complement people you know? If they are talkers and you are a listener, there may be harmony in the way the two of you relate.

On the other hand, if you are both talkers with a playful personality, be aware that some conflicts may arise if you're not patient with one another. The key to acknowledging this helpful information is to create space for different personality types. Make this a key part of your self-improvement program as you learn to better understand and relate to others.

I learned a lot in my career from Florence Littauer, a motivational speaker who spent a lifetime studying personality traits. In her book, "The Best of Florence Littauer," she states that "The first step in any type of self-improvement is to find personal areas of weakness and admit you have them. The refusal to examine our faults keeps us from doing anything positive about them."

Now that you're more knowledgeable, you can create an action plan for self- improvement. Make a mental note when a person seems to "get on your nerves." Ask yourself why. If it's a person you must interact with on a regular basis, use this information to improve your relationship. You will find there are many rewards for both of you—if nothing more than a few less headaches.

LEFT/RIGHT BRAIN CHARACTERISTICS

Understanding how humans are innately left or right brain persons helps us to grasp differences in personality, and our own unique approach to life's situations and challenges.

People who are considered left brain tend to:

- Function in a rational, intellectual and analytical manner.

- See things in logical terms and take few risks.

- Prefer spoken directions as well as writing and talking things out.

- Prefer planning and structuring.

- Often remember names.

- Like to list things and may enjoy working with numbers.

- Like thinking of one thing at a time and are sequential in nature.

Persons who are considered right brain tend to:

- Function intuitively acting freely on emotions.

- See things in a more abstract and creative way.

- Be kinesthetic learners and prefer written or demonstrated directions.

- Be creative by nature, and see and learn in pictures.

- Solve problems by looking at the whole and think simultaneously.

- Prefer to draw and handle objects, and are likely to take risks.

- Inclined to remember faces and are often musical.

Understanding differences is complex, yet simple. It's important not to be short-sighted and think a person is uncaring or too emotional when they behave in an expected manner. We innately carry traits and characteristics that are not chosen, but inborn. Let's look at some common misconceptions between men and women.

GENDER MISCONCEPTIONS

Misconceptions are based on views or opinions that are incorrect due to faulty thinking or understanding. When it comes to male-female relationships, unfair put-downs are numerous. Perhaps the key to unanimity is appreciating and recognizing our differences. It's interesting to see that married couples will ordinarily choose their opposites in personality characteristics. The blend makes for a wonderful balance to bring wholeness to the relationship as well as some major headaches!

As I mentioned earlier, our temperament is what we are born with. Our behavior is oftentimes a combination of our hormonal make-up as men and women. For example, women more often have an inclination to be nurturing, while men have a proclivity to dominate. Women are more apt to be concerned about the details of the family; while men more focused on tackling the world around them. We must understand, however, that there are variations in our world-view and tendencies according to our upbringing and exposure. For this reason, we must not be dogmatic and unyielding in our attitudes about how individuals manage their lives.

Both men and women can be misperceived and suffer from false characterizations. An example that comes to mind is the statement, "men are stronger and more competitive than women." We must be careful when making wide, brush-stroke remarks that characterize our counterparts and cause offense and tension in relationships.

I love using the scriptures for this example. The Bible says, the "people" who know their God shall be strong and do exploits. This indicates spiritual capability and is not gender specific. In this passage, scripture is characterizing the strength of character of those who "know," or are in relationship with their God—both male and female. This is affirming, and helps us understand the all-powerful potential of all God's people.

The bottom line is that sometimes we can be the reckless with our rhetoric regarding women and men. We must be careful not to stereotype so that we do not damage and ruin valued relationships.

Some of us have even been taught that women are more extravagant with money than men. Is that really true? Did you know that statistics show men incur four percent more debt than women? In my reading about the spending habits of men, I discovered that they have a tendency to buy very expensive "toys" like boats and cars.

Another interesting misconception is that, "A man ain't supposed to cry." However, women say that they respect men who show sensitivity to the hurts and concerns of others. In my view, this is not considered a weakness but shows compassion. The scriptures say that Jesus wept. If shedding tears is uncharacteristic for men, then Jesus set a poor example for his disciples.

Male and female stereotypes misrepresent our true nature. Personality differences and character flaws are neither male nor female engendered, but are inherent in human nature. As humans, we all have a need to belong and to be valued and respected.

WHAT WE ALL NEED

Abraham Maslow, a humanist psychologist, developed what we know as Maslow's Theory of Human Needs in 1943. He subsequently wrote a book entitled "Motivation and Personality" that identified a "Hierarchy of Needs." According to his findings, human needs progress upward as they are achieved:

- The need to be creative, to make a contribution and grow (self-actualization)

- The need to understand and respect myself (ego)

- The need to feel accepted, understood and respected (belonging-social)

- The need to feel safe from present or future harm and threat (security)

- The need for food, drink, warmth, shelter, etc. (survival)

Maslow initially stated that individuals must satisfy lower-level deficit needs before progressing to meet higher-level growth needs. However, he later clarified that satisfaction of a need is not an "all-or-one" phenomenon. He admitted that his earlier statements may have given "the false impression that a need must be satisfied 100 percent before the next need emerges."

Although I am not a humanist, the five basic needs listed are indeed common to us all. If I had created this list, however, I would have added the need for wholesome and caring family relationships. This key element contributes immeasurably to behavior modification and healthy personality development.

No matter our personalities or where we fall on the hierarchy of needs, we must understand the need we all have to be able to fulfill our dreams. This can only happen if we are surrounded with encouragement and people who see our potential. Cultivate an environment where people feel appreciated, respected and safe. This is not only a choice, but a responsibility we all have. When a person leaves your presence they should feel nourished—not drained and aggravated.

My friend, Dr. Loleta Foster, a clinical psychologist, once taught in her workshops that people are either toxic or nourishing. When you leave the presence of a toxic person you feel drained. When you leave the presence of a nourishing person, you feel enriched. Being understanding, accepting and even tolerant, brings people together; while being critical and judgmental is degrading. We all, male and female, deserve the dignity of personhood to freely express the best of ourselves without hurting or belittling others.

Who we are, and who we have the potential to be is incredibly complicated; yet when we began to put our personality puzzle pieces together, the results can be awe-inspiring. It's like finally finding all the pieces to grandma's "Up on The Housetop" Christmas puzzle. Even the pieces that were hidden between the pillows of the couch are important. It's time to stop merely peeking inside the box; or staring at the missing part. There's a lot more fulfillment and satisfaction in putting all the pieces together.

CHAPTER FOUR

SOCIAL SAVVY

H AVE YOU EVER met individuals who seem to personify greatness? They attract attention wherever they go and possess all the moxie it takes to command attention. They seem to relish opportunities for social engagement. There's a radiance about their countenance and a personality as bright as the sun. Connecting with others seems easy and almost effortless to them.

Well, we aren't all designed to be "social butterflies." Charismatic individuals are "people persons" who socialize well simply because they enjoy it and seem to have a knack for it. This skill is hard to analyze or teach, but when we're in the company of such individuals, we tend to notice them.

Being amiable and comfortable connecting with people on a social level is not the same as having the know how to entertain, dine or productively engage in a conversation. It's not the same as having the presence of mind to send a thank you card for a gift. The skills required to maintain great relationships is what I call, "social savvy."

This art not only requires a pleasant personality, but also calls for knowledge. It's the art of practicing good manners while entertaining, dining or simply using self-control to have a healthy conversation without being baited into gossip. Instead, you choose to be a gracious companion. No matter where we go or live, being hospitable, cordial and accommodating to others is a sign of personal refinement and essential to being socially well adjusted.

As mentioned earlier, not everyone is comfortable entertaining or connecting with others. Personal presence determines how we are perceived. Do we appear guarded and selfish, or are we comfortable conversing and receiving others into our space? Are we well-mannered and courteous, or are we abrupt, impatient and self-centered? Evaluating the way we engage is important to building wholesome relationships and is related to our ability to apply appropriate elements of the social graces.

We urgently need these lessons now. As we all know, there has been a serious breach in our cultural and moral fabric. We've already discussed the importance of spiritual and family values. Having a spiritual foundation is essential to decency, morality and the sensitivities required to build healthy relationships. When parents do not hold the line on the importance of maintaining self-respect and social civility—how can we expect teachers, law enforcement officers and civil authorities to make a difference?

Violence, civil and racial unrest has caused anarchy in our streets and neighborhoods. We need more than another law or the confiscation of guns, pepper spray and knives to bring peace and harmony. We must return to the word of God and Christian values. God so loved the world that those who believe in Him might have life and have it more abundantly. An abundant life reveals God's desire for humanity—that we enjoy tranquility and peace.

The 4th chapter of Ephesians reminds us that the life we now hold in the kingdom of God requires us to walk in unity. It teaches us that those who walk in disunity have their understanding darkened and are alienated from the life of God. We are further admonished to abandon our former behaviors (before knowing Christ) of lying, anger and corrupt communication. Ephesians 4:32 ends the chapter with the perfect summary:

"And be kind one to another, tenderhearted, forgiving one another, even as God for Christ's sake hath has forgiven you."

Chapter 5 of Ephesians, verses 1 & 2 further communicates the plan of God for social engagement:

"Be followers of God as dear children and walk in love, as Christ also hath loved us and gave himself for us an offering and a sacrifice to God for a sweetsmelling savour." The term "sweetsmelling savour" simply reminds us that our lives should be a sweet and fragrant reminder that the Lord is present. Jesus sacrificed his life to impact relationships here on earth.

Although basic policies and laws establish rules for our day-to-day manner of life, to address the core of lawlessness, we must address the heart, which the word of God says is desperately wicked.

I find it interesting that pastors and leaders in the kingdom of God want to approach immorality, racism, poverty, pornography, homelessness, sex trafficking and other social ills through government programs and political rhetoric. The solutions do not totally lie in our town halls, the courts or in the white house. We must return to biblical standards of truth.

Biblical culture was not too different than ours—the times have not really changed. Dark and sinister minds permeated the marketplace and the streets. The ruling class wanted to silence every mouth that spoke of Christ. After all, culture has only two classes of people—those who profess Christ and those who do not. The word of God reminds us as believers what our responsibility is to those who do not believe—and what his response would be. II Chronicles 7:14 KJV:

"If my people, which are called by my name, shall humble themselves, and pray and seek my face, and turn from their wicked ways; then will I hear from heaven, and will forgive their sin, and will heal their land."

In the New Testament, Paul was a prophetic voice God used in Biblical times to herald His message of hope and healing for social discord and unrest.

Ephesians 4:17 & 18 (NIV) I tell you this, insist on this in the Lord that you no longer live as the Gentiles (unbelievers) do in the futility of their thinking. They are darkened in their understanding and separated from the life of God because of the ignorance that is in them due to the hardening of their hearts. Having lost all sensitivity, they have given themselves over to sensuality so as to indulge in every kind of impurity, with a continual lust for more.

The scriptures teach us the irrefutable keys to social discourse. At the root of discord and unrest is pride. It causes hard heartedness and a disregard for the rule of law and the rights of others. The result is anarchy and unrest. It leads to sensuality and a disregard for others. We selfishly disregard our neighbor and those who have rule and authority in culture and society. The result is anarchy and unrest.

Manners have a root source—it means to manage well. A believer lives to maneuver (manage) the wrong thing so that it becomes right, in order that we may all live together in peace and harmony—oneness. God is love. The outcome of love is unity.

Let's look at the history of manners and its evolution in our Western way of life, including an overview of basic courtesies and considerations that are important in modern culture. We'll discuss the "art of tea," social introductions, thank you notes, and a reminder about managing anger, which can derail everything we've learned about personal demeanor.

Cultivate tact, for it is the mark of culture, the lubricant of human relationships, softening contacts and minimizing friction.
–Baltasar Gracian

A BRIEF HISTORY LESSON

When our country was established, it had "rules to live by" that were the standard customs of society practiced by the elite. Children were taught rules of acceptable behavior in manners and etiquette. The rules of etiquette were observed and required by "polite society."

George Washington wrote 110 "Rules of Civility & Decent Behavior," based on a 16th century set of French maxims. Most dealt with simple manners—"Cleanse not your teeth with the tablecloth, napkin, fork or knife"—Rule 100. But others formed a guide of modest and appropriate behavior in public that our first President followed. Although tablecloths were a standard home accessory during the time of George Washington, much of that has changed in modern times.

When I was growing up, Emily Post provided the go-to documentation of what was acceptable and unacceptable in society. She made this statement in one of her writings: "Whenever two people come together and their behavior affects one another, you have etiquette."

IMAGE AND ETIQUETTE DEFINED

Etiquette is the bedrock of civility in culture and society. It is a foundation for courtesy, self-respect and good manners. Recognizing and capitalizing on polite behavior builds stability in relationships. When there's care and concern for the affairs of others, healthy families and communities can thrive and grow. Unfortunately, in modern society, we also see examples of professionals who fail to comply with standards of polite and respectful behavior.

As media pundits rudely yell and talk over each other, I wonder how we've advanced in technology at the expense of losing our self-respect and dignity. Who persuaded members of our society to lay down the golden rule in exchange for a professional grandstand?

Generations come and go; however, one thing remains: Courtesy counts! This means honoring the thoughts and feelings of others. We must ask ourselves, how does my behavior show courtesy and respect in this particular situation? In every language and culture, polite behavior is regarded as a key to success, both at home and in public places.

I've spent years teaching and training on image, protocol and etiquette. What do these terms mean? How are personal relationships impacted by our knowledge of what is appropriate and considerate?

- **Image**—The definition of image simply means to "reflect the likeness of." Scripture uses this word first in Genesis 1:26: "Then God said, Let us make man in our image, in our likeness, and let them rule ..." The image maker had in mind for his created ones – that's us – to rule and manage over all the earth.

In a professional sense, I was trained first as a model and then as a coach and trainer in the field of personal and professional development. The study of image as a business or profession allows individuals to explore and specialize in key concepts that influence business and social behavior. This includes meetings management, business and social dining etiquette, public speaking, customer service skills, personal styling, color analysis, shopping services, decorating, weddings, event management and more.

- **Protocol**—The art of diplomacy; a code of guidelines and rules set for business, religious, diplomatic, military service or social life enabling an atmosphere of cooperation and mutual respect. In "Origins and their Romantic Stories," Wilfred Funk states that the word "protocol" *originally meant the first "protos" or glue*. It was a copy of the original draft that outlined the rules of an official treaty or document. Later, the word came to mean the rules of etiquette for the diplomatic corps. It signified the "first etiquette rules" that became applicable in society. Today, protocol is said to be the "glue" or conduct that holds a civil society together.

  In a secular and spiritual sense, I love the fact that protocol is essentially "the glue" and first rules that holds society together. How can we manage our homes without them? How do we manage our classrooms, businesses, corporate boardrooms and government without them? Manners and protocol lay our foundations to human discourse.

- **Etiquette**—The art of gracious and considerate behavior; rules of conduct expected and required in business and social life. Sometimes called "civility training," it embodies behavioral standards and cultural norms passed down through generations.

I might also add that protocol and etiquette are both rooted in a sound knowledge and practice of human relations. Oftentimes, after being hired on a new position, a person will be given an office procedures manual. The office hours, dress code and other standards of office operation and expectations will be included. The manual sets the ground rules for individuals to be able to work together cooperatively, as well to establish an atmosphere of courtesy and mutual respect.

When an individual learns the discipline of a more correct way of doing things, the correct way becomes as easy as our old habit once was. Good manners taught at home are essential. When a woman or man instructs their children and grandchildren on the rules of manners and etiquette, a strong foundation is being built for positive self-esteem and how to build respectful relationships with others or generations to come.

"Tend one garden and you will birth worlds."
–Kate Braverman

I believe that a woman's life, marriage and family are her most important "garden." Prioritizing and staying focused here is paramount. Not only are we providing a good example as a role model, but teaching manners and etiquette has a ripple effect. Acts of goodwill and kindness will inevitably impact all we manage. A tranquil garden brings peace of mind.

MANNERS & ETIQUETTE–THE BIBLICAL CONTEXT

Because *The Get Noticed Woman* is written to all women, but, women in the body of Christ in particular, I will now set the context for the term "manners" from a biblical context.

During biblical times, in the Old Testament, the book of Leviticus outlines standards of dress, diet and behavior. The standards of decorum and civility were also called "manners." There were standards of behavior for singles, widows and married couples. God's people were warned that there was to be a difference between His people and those of other nations. They were not to conduct their manner of living as others—worshipping other Gods. They were to give their love, honor and respect to one God—the creator of the heavens and earth. This way, they would enjoy the unity, peace and harmony God promised.

Leviticus 20:23:
And ye shall not walk in the manners (customs, lifestyle) of the nation which I cast out before you, for they committed all these things and therefore I was abhorred (wearied and grieved) by them.

For some sins or disobedience, the penalty was death. Some examples were disrespect of parents, adultery, incest, homosexuality, and cohabiting with a beast. Others would suffer barrenness for their sin. Thank God for the age of grace. In the life of the New Testament church, we have been freed from the curse of the law. Jesus Christ paid for our sin and trespasses through his death and resurrection.

Leviticus 20:26:
And you shall be holy unto me: for I the Lord am holy, and have severed you from other people, that you should be mine.

Jesus took upon himself the sins of the world. Consequently, the "letter of the law" was lifted. Redemption was made available for all humankind. The curse of the law gave way to the love of God in Christ Jesus, so that instead of separation, we can enjoy unity in the spirit with those who accept him as Lord. As a Father, God states here that, "you are mine." God's eternal dream and desire is that all his creation, by the freedom of their will accept him as a Father which brings us in unity with his plan and will.

He loves us and understands all of our weaknesses. Our Christian duty is to follow His example.

Hebrews 4:15 & 16:
For we have not a high priest which cannot be touched with the feeling
of our infirmities (sins and weaknesses); but was in all points tempted
like as we are, yet without sin. Let us therefore come boldly unto the
throne of grace that we may obtain mercy, and find grace to help in
time of need.

According to the Pew Research Center, a nonpartisan research group, in 2017, about 71% of Americans identify as Christians. As a Christian myself, the reason I write, is with the intent to release God's love. I want to encourage those who don't know God's love or the tenets of the Christian faith, to learn and grow in their understanding of God and his love.

At the core of the Christian belief is the significance of coming together to dine—just as Jesus did with his disciples. This is where we can kick off our shoes, relax around a meal and even share some laughter. The timeless truth we share based on biblical truth is priceless. Love does not hold grudges and is forgiving. At these times, we find reconciliation with a brother or sister. The significance of sharing and caring while sipping a cup of tea without a care in the world is one of life's greatest treasures.

In many parts of the world—Asia, Africa and Europe—and in other cultures, "tea time" is like a daily ritual. I have found that when I don't know a person, being asked to have a cup of tea with them is heart-warming. As I meet women and men, not only from the states, but, from other cultures, I've found that sharing a cup of tea or coffee signals good will and encourages well-meaning conversation. This not only warms the heart, but the tummy as well.

THE ART OF TEA

The USA is called a melting pot because it has been shaped by Native Americans, Europeans, Africans, Latin Americans and Asians. Because all these cultures have significantly contributed to our culture, religion and food; our traditions are diversified.

We are the 3rd largest country in the world with a population of about 325 million people. The US is considered to be one of the most culturally diverse countries in the world. The challenge to learn to connect with other nationalities is readily available—especially when enrolled in a culturally diverse school or when attending a church that offers multicultural worship experiences.

I learned a number of years ago, that sipping on a cup of tea or coffee is a great way to connect when people don't know one another. I had a friend named, Karen, a number of years ago from Great Britain. She taught me how significant a cup of tea can be, not just for personal enjoyment, but, in a social and relationship building context.

I once visited Manchester, England and found that understanding "the art of tea" was a given. I've chosen to share with you the process.

Tea, of course, is a hot beverage made with water and tea leaves. It's enjoyed by many people throughout Great Britain, the Middle East, and African countries where it's customary to have tea on a daily basis. It would be considered rude for an invited guest to refuse this gesture of hospitality. After all, in some African and Middle Eastern countries, it would be considered rude to refuse this gesture of hospitality.

In your own home, on special occasions, the finest cloth or linen napkins and china can be used to show guests honor and respect. Add a touch of celebration by using a center-piece of fresh flowers. Plastic or silk flowers aren't considered acceptable for special occasions— including taking tea.

Fill an empty kettle with fresh, cold water. Tap water is acceptable for most purposes, but a truly great cup of tea starts with filtered or spring water. The more oxygen in your water, the better the tea will taste. Never use distilled water, or previously-boiled water. Next, use bags or loose tea with a strainer. Let the bags or strainer steep for a few minutes before discarding. Steeping is allowing your tea to sit in the water to make it stronger. You'll want to have sweeteners like sugar or honey for guests to use.

For some, it's also customary to add milk. If you use milk or cream, pour it in the cup first. If you don't care for cream, make it available for others. When sugar is used, serving it in cubed form adds a touch of elegance. The sugar will go into the cup before the tea is poured. A tiny teaspoon for stirring adds extra elegance. Serving a dessert such as cookies, crumpets, shortbread or other sweets will make your get-together extra special. You may even add gourmet candies, caramel and fudge as a special treat.

Now it's time to enjoy. As we know, conversation never goes out of style. Neither will coffee and tea. Wherever those are brewing, you'll find laughter, a joke or two, and engaging gab. That's why Starbucks or Panera are important gathering places in today's culture. We love the simplicity of sipping and discussing the last episode from a sitcom or movie, and the ease of doing nothing but enjoying another's company.

Conversations lead to solving the challenges of late school buses, overbearing supervisors, or even putting a dream back on track. Don't forget to have your cup today.

WHAT SHALL I WEAR?

Because social environments have gone almost strictly casual, more than ever, individuals can relax regarding what is or is not appropriate to wear. It is, however, important on certain occasions to ask the host or hostess if there is a dress code.

For instance, when an individual is celebrating a milestone in life such as weddings, anniversary celebrations, retirement, birthday parties, always look your best. Even when you are going to play tennis or flag football, a wrinkled shirt is never appropriate.

Of course, current fads take jeans everywhere, however, well dressed men and women know that jeans are not appropriate for a formal event. In some cases jeans cannot be worn in business offices with the exception of "dress down days."

Listed below are a number of dress code guidelines to help you prepare for most occasions. We've included what is appropriate attire for gentlemen because it's not unusual for a man to inquire or seek guidance when escorting a lady to an event. We also understand that some men are even more particular about their appearance than women. At any rate, being familiar with key categories of appropriate dress is important. Note the following when going to special events:

Formal—Ladies should wear a long gown or a tea-length party dress. Gentlemen should wear a dark suit or tuxedo.

Semi-formal—Ladies should wear a party outfit; a dressy dress or slacks. Gentlemen should wear a dark suit or a sports coat with a dressy shirt.

Informal—Ladies can wear business best or dress up according to the occasion. Gentlemen can wear dress slacks, dress shirts or a suit.

Black tie—Ladies can wear a tea-length or long party dress. Gentlemen must wear a tuxedo.

White tie—Ladies can wear a formal gown or a sleeveless gown. Gentlemen should wear a tailcoat with matching trousers.

Casual—Ladies can wear stylish or designer jeans and a casual top or a comfortable dress, skirt and blouse. Gentlemen can dress down and wear jeans, a cotton or polo shirt or sweater. No business jacket or suit is required.

Dressy casual—Ladies can wear a comfortable dressy outfit in either a dress, skirt or slacks is appropriate. Gentlemen can wear long slacks and a dress shirt and or jacket of any fabric or style according to the occasion.

Business Casual—This look is designed to place emphasis on attracting entrepreneurs and those who are engaged and working in the marketplace. It's more relaxed than casual and more like "dressy casual" with no business overtones. A comfortable dress, skirt or classic jeans with a business top and jacket would be appropriate.

SHOWING UP CONFIDENT...THE RULE OF 12'S

Your first impression counts. Make sure you show up confident, especially when meeting someone professionally or when you are meeting someone for the first time. Although masks have become appropriate—for who knows how long, use wisdom and try to make sure you are cautious and considerate at all times. Note, I didn't say fearful, but, use sound judgement.

Most importantly, wherever you go, make sure you ask questions before you arrive so that you are aware of what is expected related to masks, social distancing or other social matters. You will feel more self-assured when you follow these guidelines.

Make certain the:

- First 12 steps that you take when you enter the room... the interview... the banquet or wherever you are going... are 12 confident steps. Walk with authority, purpose and presence. Don't drag your feet. When you sit, don't slouch. Sit tall with your feet on the floor.

If you decide to cross your legs, cross at the knee taking care to slant legs, knees and feet to the side for a poised look.

- First 12 inches of your body from the shoulders-down show impeccable grooming. Your face is the focal point of your body. Make certain your face and hair communicate excellence in grooming. No dandruff, hair, spills or lint should be seen on the shoulders.

- First 12 words you speak are complimentary. Show thanks and appreciation, even if you have to share disturbing or unpleasant information. Also, if the room is decorated nicely, or this is your first invitation, make a pleasant remark about your visit.

MAKING INTRODUCTIONS

Social distancing has complicated the common courtesy of shaking hands when being introduced. Although extending the right hand for a firm hand shake is customary, I suggest smiling with a nod to acknowledge the other person or clasping the hands together with a slight bow—if the individual does not choose to shake hands. Simply lifting the right hand to say, "Hi," with a slight nod of the head is also a polite gesture.

Reading body language is important. If a person is an acquaintance, friend or relative and would like to hug, you should only comply if you choose to do so. If you do not know the person, mirror their motions. If they want to touch elbows or simply smile—do the same. The final choice is yours. Do not allow for intimidation, coercion or pressure to act in any way that is uncomfortable for you.

TRADITIONAL HAND SHAKING

If a person would like to shake hands and you are comfortable doing so, comply. Here are the traditional and acceptable ways to shake hands and make introductions:

- When being introduced, extend your hand and clearly state your full name (first and last). If you are sitting, stand for the introduction.

- A firm handshake is important. Extend your hand for a web-to-web connection with the thumb-up. Only a couple of firm, well-meaning shakes are appropriate. "Knuckle-grips," hammering motions or using two-hands is uncomfortable and considered rude.

- In a social setting, a lady is not required to shake hands. She may simply smile and nod to acknowledge the introduction. If the person is a personal friend, she may choose to hug them.

- A gentleman should stand to greet a lady when she enters the room for the first time. If she re-enters, standing is not necessary.

- Never sit while being introduced to someone standing. In a social setting, introduce males to females (meaning the female's name is spoken first). "Angela, this is my friend, Carl Bowing. Carl, this is Angela Casey."

- Introduce the younger person to an elder person: "Grandmother, this is my friend, Shannon Owens. Shannon, this is my grandmother, Lela White."

- After the introduction, say something that will allow easy conversation between the newly introduced persons, i.e., "Candace is in my math class and we're also members of the local debate team."

- Introduce a non-official person to an official person: "Mayor Sherman, this is my principal, Cheryl Washington. Ms. Washington, this is Mayor Donald Sherman." Remember the name of the person with a title or an honorary position such as a pastor, public or political official is always spoken first.

- When introducing persons standing or sitting in a group, randomly choose the person to start with, then introduce each person in the order they are seated or standing. Never skip around to imply some people are more important than others.

- Make eye contact when you say a person's name. If you don't remember a person's name, apologize and say, for example, "I'm sorry, I know we've met before, but I don't recall your name."

- If you see that a person is struggling to recall your name, be polite and help them by quickly speaking up as soon as you notice.

- To help you remember names the next time, try making associations with the person's name while mentally repeating the name several times to lock-it in your memory. For instance, if the person's name is Cameron Brown, think of a camera sitting on top of your favorite brown shoes.

- There are also times when we must introduce an individual who is not from our culture or country. During these times, be sure to listen carefully to better understand a heavy accent or dialect. Be polite and smile.

INTRODUCING AND ADDRESSING FOREIGN OFFICIALS

In the U.S. we use the titles Ms., Miss or Mrs. for women, followed by their surname. When we are uncertain of a woman's title, it is polite to use the title "Madame," meaning "my lady." This term is known by the French as a title of diplomacy throughout the world. If you have difficulty pronouncing a last name, simply saying "Madame" is polite and acceptable.

When addressing heads of state, cabinet officers, ambassadors, high ranking officials in America "The Honorable" is used in front of a person's surname to note the importance of their present or former position.

For heads of state, ambassadors, cabinet officers of other countries and high-ranking members of the clergy, it is proper to use "His Excellency" or "Her Excellency" before the given name or surname.

BEING SOCIALLY AWARE

- When you enter a room and you're a guest, wait until your host gestures where you are to be seated. Do not always assume you can take any seat that may seem available. There are times when dad has a favorite chair or a particular seat is being reserved for a special guest.

- Whoever arrives first at a door—male or female should hold it open for others following behind. Keep it open until all have passed through. Younger persons should try to move quickly to get the door for older persons.

- At swinging and rotating doors, the host or hostess should go first so that he or she can direct activities on the other side.

- When a lady is escorted by a gentleman, he offers her his left arm. She gently places her right hand on the inside of his upper arm or left elbow, as opposed to just linking arms. He does not pull her along. They should walk in step together.

- When walking outside along a street, the gentleman walks curb-side to protect the lady from traffic, mud splashing, etc. If the two cannot pass an area side-by-side, the gentleman hands the lady forward and follows her single file. If there is an obstruction or a physically challenging area, the gent goes first and offers a strong hand to his companion.

- It is not good manners to chew gum in public. Use breath mints instead. If you must chew because mints are not available, be very discreet—no one should know.

- When someone says, "Hello, how are you?" make eye contact and greet them in an affirming way. Because this is a rhetorical question, you will want to refrain from mentioning anything negative like your headache.

- If you've met the person before, try to initiate conversation with those in your company by mentioning the time and place you were last together as a conversation starter. "I think we met at Renee's birthday party. Have you spoken with her lately?"

- Sharing a polite and friendly compliment is a great conversation starter: "I really like your jacket. It looks great on you."

- Know when you're boring someone. It is rude to do all the talking. Pause to allow others to speak.

- Be a good listener and don't interrupt or indicate impatience by frequently checking your watch.

- It is rude to whisper in the presence of others and make side comments.

- When at a party or social event, it is rude to pair off with one person you know for the duration of the evening without attempting to get acquainted with others.

- Do not complete a person's sentence for them. Try to avoid checking the time or your cell phone while conversing with others. This shows a lack of interest.

- Always smile and speak when passing. Although you may not know the person, this is considered a gesture of courtesy.

- Never make a scene by laughing loudly, using foul language or showing poor taste in telling jokes.

- Never correct someone publically. This is obviously embarrassing. Speak with them in private.

- When you are someone's guest at an event, show appreciation for having been invited and follow their lead.

- Don't talk about money, health, your diet or ask overly personal questions.

- When you are in public, keep a check on your facial expressions and emotions. If your spouse is late for the party and your children are being noisy, deal with them in a positive way. Keep smiling.

- When you are in a public place and a senior person arrives, be willing to give up your seat, even if the men and others around you are not courteous enough to do so.

- If others are in your immediate space while conversing with someone, try to include everyone in the conversation so that no one feels excluded.

- When sharing your opinion, try to avoid political, racial, religious or other sensitive issues.

- Never arrive at a social event without greeting the person who invited you. If that person happens to be different from the host or hostess, make sure to greet this person too.

- When it is time to leave, it's important to say goodbye and thank the person who invited you or your host before departing. Try to comment favorably on the time spent with them.

- If you are a house guest, take a gift or leave a gift of thanks. The longer you stay, the more generous the gift should be. If you are a relative and visit often, leaving a note of thanks is always appropriate.

- If you have an overnight guest, welcome them with flowers, a box of candy or a fruit basket and a welcome notecard in their room.

- No matter where you go, leave the area or space better than the way you found it. This means, if you stay overnight, it's helpful to take-out your trash, hang up towels, and make your bed. No one expects you to vacuum or scrub the bathroom. However, be careful not to leave a mess.

- Your children are never too young to begin learning social courtesies that you observe and practice.

INVITATIONS

It is acceptable to make a phone call to invite guests over for an informal occasion. Close friends don't need a written invitation. However, if you receive a written invitation to a party, picnic, bridal shower or some other special event, always RSVP within a week of receiving the invitation and certainly before the deadline. Never ask to bring a date or escort unless the words "and guest" appear on the invitation or RSVP card.

There are times when you may receive an invitation while an unexpected guest is visiting or perhaps the host isn't aware that you're engaged and you want to invite an escort. When this is the case, ask permission. Simply call the host and explain the circumstances so the extra name can be added to the guest list.

When shopping for the right invitations, choose quality paper stock. Remember, your invitations represent and announce your taste in presentation and style. Make certain they represent you well.

THE RSVP

The acronym "RSVP" is often found at the end of an invitation. This notation was derived from the French phrase "Répondez s'il vous plait" (respond if you please) or "reply if you please." In using this term, the guest is requested to reply by a certain date.

It is courteous to respond within two days and no longer than 7-10 days before the event. This allows the host or hostess to adequately prepare food and drink for the appropriate number of guests. "Regrets Only" is another way for soliciting a reply and is usually followed by a telephone number.

SAYING THANK YOU

Writing a "thank you" note is an important step to remember after being invited to a special event, when receiving a special gift or when someone does a special favor. Sending a text or email is fine for small favors; however, there are times when someone will go out of their way spending time and money to be a blessing. In this case, taking the time to select and send a special card is appropriate—even if they only live down the street from you.

We never want to take for granted those who remember us in special ways. Showing kindness elicits admiration, respect and makes a positive impression every time.

When you make intentional efforts to practice good manners, your children will notice. I intentionally chose to include a photo here—because now days, it is rare to see displays of kindness and courtesy. There are times when parents relegate writing thank you notes to something girls should do. This is far from the truth.

Be knowledgeable and intentional about showing young people the correct way to say please and thank you, as well as how to write thank you notes. When writing correspondence, it is important to know the forms of address.

Use the correct title

When writing thank you notes and other correspondence, be sure to use a title. A title is used on correspondence of any kind unless the person is a peer or a very close friend. Acceptable titles are:

- Mr., Mrs., Miss, Ms. or a professional title. Miss is often used for a young lady age 12 and under. Ms. is used for teens and women who don't specify marital status in their personal or business lives. Mrs. is used for personal and business women who prefer to use it.

- Widows of professional persons continue to be addressed as when their husband was living. Ex: Mrs. Fulton Holt or if they prefer, Mrs. Shelly Holt. It is fine to ask what they prefer.

- When a deceased person must be mentioned on a list, the person is listed as: The Late Allen L. Singleton.

- When addressing a lawyer use: "Sarah R. Campbell, Esq." In this country, Esq. in the abbreviated form is used as a matter of choice after the surname of a lawyer for both males and females. Esq. is never used, however, when writing a social invitation to a couple, one or both whom might be lawyers.

- When one or both are doctors, use: Dr. and Mrs. Samuel Cannon or Dr. Florence Smith and Mr. Larry Smith or Dr. Florence Smith and Dr. Larry Smith.

- When both are Reverends use: The Reverends Forest & Clarissa Ball or The Reverends Mr. and Mrs. Forest Ball.

- When a man uses Jr. after his surname, it signifies that his father is alive and has the exact same name. If the two men live in the same household, the father will usually use Sr. after his surname. When the father dies, the son will eventually drop the Jr. because the distinction is no longer needed.

- A man named after his father who is a "Jr." is called, "the third," usually written as Roman numeral III. A child named after his uncle or grandfather becomes "the 2nd" or "II."

Writing Your Thank You Note

Being courteous enough to say "thank you" when a colleague is nice enough to share one of her granola bars during lunchtime is certainly commendable. On the other hand, when a colleague is thoughtful enough to purchase a scarf to acknowledge your birthday, you must remember to do more than just say "thanks," but to show your appreciation in writing. It is rude to receive a gift without following through with this special gesture.

It is also rude to accept an invitation and attend celebrations like birthday, wedding, anniversary, retirement parties without bringing a gift. If the honoree is a close friend, you are expected to send a gift if you cannot attend.

When you make intentional efforts to practice good manners, your children will notice. Also be intentional about showing them the correct way to say please and thank you, as well as, how to write thank you notes.

Here are a few guidelines to follow when writing thank you notes:

- Paragraph 1: Greet the person and thank him or her. Don't forget to mention the amount of money or what gift you received. For example, "Thank you for my new pen set," or "Thank you for the $20 for my birthday."

- Paragraph 2: Make a comment about how special your gift is or how you will use the gift, i.e., "The $20 will help me reach my goal for buying a new laptop by the end of summer."

- Paragraph 3: Make closing remarks and wish them well. Don't forget to use a complimentary close, such as "Best Regards," and sign your name.

There are many courtesies people really appreciate. My friend, Stanley Reahard's mom was a woman with scores of admirers—including me. She wrote a book which I treasure, Words of Wisdom by Annabel. Here is a quote from her book.

Ask people over—they like the attention. Write thank you notes quickly.
–Annabel Smith

Because connecting socially isn't always pleasant, I have found my list of "cool downs" helpful. We all have unpleasant moments—times when we need time and space to regroup.

TWELVE WAYS TO COOL DOWN

Social savvy requires keeping a level head and being in control of your emotions at all times—even when it's difficult to do so. There are times when letting off steam by giving a person a piece of your mind would seem appropriate. However, being tactful and patient under pressure will prove to be more profitable in the end.

Losing your temper or ending up in a disagreement is never intentional. However, getting embroiled in a dispute or confrontational matter can easily destroy an individual's personal and public image. Because an unforeseen encounter is possible at any time, practicing how to handle potential land-mines is wise.

When things aren't going our way or when someone ruffles our feathers, we must find ways to tactfully address the situation. Take a deep breath before you speak. Replace negative thoughts with positive ones.

To handle yourself, use your head. To handle others, use your heart.
–Eleanor Roosevelt

There are 12 ways to manage your emotions so that you can remain reasonably calm during stressful and challenging times:

- If possible, remove yourself from the situation to take time and think things through.

- Listen to your favorite music, something calming or soothing. You may even choose to hum or sing along.

- Drink a glass of cold water or a non-carbonated beverage.

- Concentrate on the big picture. Sometimes you have to choose your battles. This one may not be worth the energy to get involved.

- Take a walk and enjoy nature.

- Exercise by jogging or swimming.

- Write down your feelings before responding to a contentious text or an email.

- Before trying to convince someone that they are wrong—think again. Remember they think they're right and probably won't change their opinion.

- Take responsibility for your actions and quickly apologize if you're wrong.

- Attack the problem and not the person.

- If you must follow through with action, do so after you've had a chance to think things through.

- It may be wise to get advice from a trusted mentor or someone who can share another point of view.

HANDLING CONFLICT

When socializing and connecting with others, we can all agree that it is important to master two very important skills—self-control and conflict management. We cannot ignore the fact that we will not always understand or agree with the opinion or behavior of others.

Quiet time and a consult with the Holy Spirit is key during times like this. Romans 12:1-3 admonishes us to be transformed by the renewing of our minds—not following the pattern of those who do not know God. In this way, we will be able to test and prove what God's good and perfect will is in each and every situation.

Renewing (evaluating our thought processes in order to become agreeable to change) requires us to reconsider how we've always managed certain situations to acquire new habits. This process requires humility of mind carried out in the spirit of love.

Romans 12:9-16:
Love must be sincere. Hate what is evil; cling to what is good. Be devoted to one another in (brotherly and sisterly) love. Honor one another above yourselves. ...be joyful in hope, patient in affliction, faithful in prayer. Share with God's people who are in need. Practice hospitality.

Bless those who persecute you; bless and do not curse. Rejoice with those who rejoice; mourn with those who mourn.

Live in harmony with one another. Do not be proud, but be willing to associate with people of low position. Do not be conceited.

Sometimes handling conflict and rude behavior will rear its ugly head in the form of personal insults—misunderstandings and more. We can all identify impolite behavior when we see it. However, the same is true when we are personally guilty. It is good to become a master at exercising self-control so that harmful behaviors do not master us. Some examples of rude behavior are:

- Blaming
- Name calling
- Threats
- Putdowns

- Bullying
- Lying
- Profanity
- Exaggerating
- Choosing not to listen
- Retaliation
- Accusations
- Showing jealousy or anger
- Embarrassing others

Ask yourself, "How do I handle conflict?" Take this 5-point test and see how many points you earn.

- I am considerate of others' feelings and ignore insulting behavior.

- I don't find it difficult to apologize when I've offended.

- I don't show jealousy but find ways to celebrate the accomplishments of others.

- I find ways to compliment before pointing out a problem.

- I am a forgiving and understanding person who can overlook inappropriate and insulting behavior, especially when I understand that no harm was intended.

WINNING WORDS

Remember this statement when trying to reframe your thinking...

Most people are about as happy as they make up their minds to be.
–Abraham Lincoln

As we close this chapter on social etiquette, here are some "winning words" that will always make a positive impression wherever we go:

One very important word... PLEASE

Two important words... THANK YOU

Three important words...MAY I HELP?

Four important words... WHAT IS YOUR OPINION?

Five important words... YOU DID A GOOD JOB

Six important words... I ADMIT I MADE A MISTAKE

In summary, what is social savvy? It's showing others that we care. It's about showing kindness. It's going out of our way to be gracious and understanding. Acting in these ways allows our family, friends and colleagues to see us at our very best. Most assuredly, we will gain the admiration, respect and godly attention we deserve.

BUSINESS ETIQUETTE

I N THE ERA of "social distancing" the common business and social hand-shake is under fierce attack. One might ask, "Should I bow, do a fist-bump, smile and nod or simply wave?" Others will want to tap elbows, which I personally think can be quite awkward when a person like myself attempts to link up with her six-feet-seven-inch tall son-in-law. It is best during challenging times like these, to evaluate our professional environments and comply with required mandates on the job.

This is one of those topics that dozens of social, spiritual and professional "experts" will find reason to disagree on what is and is not appropriate. After you consider and comply with the laws, statutes and mandates of your city, state, place of business, etc., the choice of how and when you socialize becomes very personal.

As a futuristic fashionista, I can see a possible introduction of designer gloves into the professional arena. It is possible that women, in particular may add gloves to their everyday business attire—not only for the purpose of "social distancing," but, to add an interesting flare to the daily routine. Especially those who are in the field of sales—or those who travel frequent.

Wearing masks and gloves (optional) to stay personally safe in public and professional places makes sense. This is also a practical, sensible and courteous gesture to put others at ease. Even though you may personally feel comfortable, there is always the possibility of facing the person who wants to stand 10 feet away from anything or anyone breathing.

My final comment about social distancing is this. Never allow others to impose their perceived liberties or restrictions on you. This is *your* life. Freedoms are guaranteed both in Christ and under our Constitution. Above all, we must exercise freedom over fear to be true to our calling as ambassadors for the Lord Jesus Christ. Wisdom is the principal thing, the word of God tells us. Therefore, we must apply wisdom to this and every matter of significance.

Proverbs 8:10-12: Choose my instruction instead of silver, knowledge rather than choice gold, for wisdom is more precious than rubies. I wisdom, dwell together with prudence; I possess knowledge and discretion.

Understanding business etiquette skills is key to navigating the professional scene with confidence and credibility. People do business with people they like, trust and respect. The way you dress, behave and present yourself to prospective clients and associates when transacting business can make or break a deal.

Whether you're engaging one-on-one with the company's vice president, or with an external client, there are rules of behavior in the workplace and expectations of respect and camaraderie that are required to sustain a healthy work environment.

In this chapter, you'll find powerful, yet, simple keys to enhance your business networking and non-verbal communication skills. You'll learn how to accelerate and optimize your career goals, how to confidently dine in professional environments and much more.

In today's market, employees and entrepreneurs must embrace basic and specific people skills to stand out from their peers. Enjoying this competitive advantage means more than simply showing ambition and displaying a will to win. On the contrary. Workplace excellence also means more than "paying your dues" by working long hours—while begrudging the time lost with family and friends.

Letitia Baldrige, the American etiquette expert, who served as Jacqueline Kennedy's Social Secretary, made this statement in her book "Letitia Baldridge's Complete Guide to Executive Manners:"

"An awareness of good manners *automatically* propels human beings in the affirmative direction. Up to now, management has given this subject little thought, particularly in how it relates to profit. It's time to think about and give it priority attention in management training."

In a nationwide analysis of managers, women measured low in confidence and presence, while rating higher than males in organizational skills, goal setting and motivating others. This may be because women were often placed in roles that didn't allow them to maximize their full potential. For this reason, they frequently lack the necessary support to confidently fulfill more challenging roles.

While it's important to consider the keys to competence in building better business relationships, we should also discuss some prevailing mental blocks that may impede our success. Let's consider chivalrous behavior, for example. For decades, women have rejected certain gestures offered by men as sexist and derogatory. However, chivalrous behavior could be viewed as simple acts of graciousness, honor and courtesy.

When courtesies are offered, perhaps women shouldn't be rude and disrespectful to prove a point. After all, acts of kindness coming from anyone, at any time, should be graciously received. For this reason, the following statement rings true...

> *"A gentleman will open doors, pull out chairs, and carry things, not because she's helpless or unable, but because he wants to show her that she is valuable and worthy of respect."*
> –Michael Fiore

Of course, because of gender biases, even today, being a woman in the workplace can present challenges. However, those challenges should not be met with a protest when men want to show honor or respect. Because many of us value who we are and the talent we bring to the board room and the cafeteria, we expect to be treated with consideration and held in high regard.

FEMININE ASSET MANAGEMENT

Financial asset management is a hot topic often discussed in the boardroom. However, when considering women in the workplace, it's important for us to understand the ramifications of "feminine asset management." Allow me to explain.

While visiting organizations and speaking to professional development managers, I've often observed that women who possess unique personal and professional qualities go unnoticed. Women have the ability to influence and bring about transformational change that goes far beyond their pretty smile and power suit.

Unfair biases cause discouragement and lead to nonproductive lives. To squash prejudices, women must acquire knowledge and skill to build better business relationships. This means going beyond learning the disciplines of a trade or skill to advance our careers.

GAINING THE ETIQUETTE ADVANTAGE IN CUSTOMER SERVICE

Individuals must embrace the nuances of business etiquette to land on top in today's competitive business arena. Building and maintaining better business relationships requires the "etiquette advantage." Often this simply means employing good customer service skills, which will ultimately lead to trusting relationships. Of course, this strategic move also impacts the bottom line.

Customer service is governed by "The rule of 10." It costs approximately $10,000 to get a new customer; it takes only 10 seconds to lose one, and can take 10 years to recover. (Independent Study)

What a compelling statement. This is why employers are concerned with the professional image of their employees. When women—and men, understand and believe in themselves, others will be inspired to do business with them. Gaining a competitive edge begins with the courage to step-up, and step-out of self-defeating behavior patterns.

Sheryl Sandburg, the author of *"Lean In: Women, Work and the Will to Succeed,"* has become a powerful voice to help women overcome self-defeating behaviors in the workplace. Although I don't agree with all she purports, I do agree when she challenges what many feminists believe—that women are strictly the victims of gender bias and discrimination.

Gender discrimination, of course, has been statistically proven, and is alive and well. However, often women are far too passive, give up too easily, or are willing to blame others for their failures.

Sandburg states: "Women have to prove themselves more than men. A McKinsey study says men are promoted based on potential, while women are promoted based on accomplishments." She also believes that maybe women are *holding themselves back* and... "Successful women are more likely to feel like impostors who will be found out."

So, the question is, what will it take for women to advance and excel? I certainly understand that women don't often get the "automatic vote of confidence" afforded to men in the marketplace. However, in order to have more confidence and credibility, we must take intentional steps toward self-empowerment.

Sandburg suggests, "The only way to change the game is by taking risks, choosing growth, challenging ourselves, and asking for promotions. It comes down to having more self-confidence, which is at the heart of what it means to lead..." We can never be our best when we doubt our potential and listen to negative self-talk.

Business etiquette skills give you the finesse to transition from uncertainty to clarity when working with others. We must be willing to advance professionally by taking the initiative to gain access, and come to the table where important decisions are made.

We must also become intentional about making important contributions by "leaning in" to get the job done. Once we get involved in the process, we must *stay involved* until the issue is resolved. Giving up is not an option—but, giving the attention necessary to customers and clients becomes key. We give them our best, realizing there would be no need for our expertise or services without them.

GETTING NOTICED IN THE WORKPLACE - POSITIVE BUSINESS PRESENCE

Something happened early in my career that catapulted me from an ordinary office position to working in a global world-class environment. I'm sharing it here because this is one of my never-to-be forgotten moments at work.

In 1994, my husband accepted a teaching position at Otterbein University in Westerville, Ohio. To help the family get settled, I left my new image consulting business for a salaried position with the district office of a major denomination.

Although I had considerable experience as a corporate trainer, this position required a different skillset. After working there for a couple of years, my supervisor asked me to assist her with organizing an upcoming training. To my surprise, she invited me to facilitate a workshop.

Of course, this request caused me to lean into what I had once done best. I had an excellent relationship with my supervisor by this time. She had learned to respect my judgement and often complimented me on my professional skills. I was extremely flattered by her invitation and grateful for the opportunity because non-clergy were rarely invited to facilitate workshops and training in this organization.

I remember thinking that although we may not be aware, others are watching and observing our performance. While we are simply working hard to do a good job, we get noticed. When the day for my workshop arrived, I was prepared and raring to go. The program theme focused on identifying the unique and diverse gifts and talents of pastors and leaders.

I was about ten minutes into my presentation when the door opened and a tall gentleman walked across the room and quietly sat down. His corporate look and professional demeanor was impressive. Although he hardly made a sound, he stood out from the crowd. After listening and observing my presentation for about 15 minutes, he got up and left with his cell phone in hand.

When I arrived at work the next morning, my supervisor called me and asked me if I was sitting down. Not knowing what she would say, I became a bit anxious. She asked if I noticed the gentleman who came late to my workshop. I replied, "Yes, I noticed him." She proceeded to say that he was the global training director for Procter & Gamble and was very impressed with my skills as a trainer. He had asked my supervisor about me and wanted to know if I might be interested in interviewing for an independent contracting opportunity.

I was both surprised and thrilled. I stood up from my desk with phone in hand. I took a few steps and it felt like I was walking on air. The timing was perfect. I did not know it at the time but discovered a few days later, that my office was being reorganized.

When I arrived at the P & G Global Training Center in Cincinnati, Ohio, I took my resume and offered it to the same gentleman I had observed during my earlier presentation. To my surprise, he said with a smile, "I don't need to look at it… I've seen you train." He said that hearing and seeing me was all that he needed and was confident I was the person he was looking for.

He said he was a former pastor and was attending the workshops that day to catch-up with friends and associates. He said that he left my training early because he realized he was in the wrong room. He was so impressed with my presentation that he wanted to offer me an independent contracting position with P&G as a "Team Effectiveness" and "Diversity" trainer. This position involved a significant increase in pay. In this new position, I would earn two-and-a-half times in one day, the amount I was currently earning in three-weeks. As I drove home from the interview, I was amazed at what transpired. He told me that while on assignment in my new position, a private driver would pick me up from my hotel each morning and take me home each day.

Ladies, timing is everything. As I mentioned earlier, my district office was reorganizing and my position would be phased out. Providentially, God's timing is always perfect. The position was ordained for me. It was my turn to get noticed.

My supervisor was elated for me, but not surprised. She said, since first meeting me she thought I was far more capable of doing greater things. I knew her belief in me was one of the reasons I excelled in my position. She has since passed away, but was an excellent mentor and friend.

As I mentioned. Although we don't always realize it, our supervisors and associates are taking notice of our performance—even when we are doing what we believe are routine or mundane tasks. They may not say much, but just when the time is right, you may be rewarded for what I call "positive business presence."

A close friend of mine, Evon Hughes, gave me a poster that expresses why I believe I flourished and grew in that environment. The poster says, "Like Flowers on a windowsill, the human spirit leans toward the sunshine of freedom, for that is where we bloom the best." The value of working with individuals who believe in you is like water to a thirsty plant on a hot summer day. It's rejuvenating and refreshing, and provides the impetus to grow. I believe that when people work in an environment of criticism and lack of trust, they should consider pulling up their roots to find a more wholesome place to grow.

Because many of us are in a toxic environment, we develop symptoms of anxiety and depression. Our health begins to suffer that can lead to a downward spiral in our career. It is better to take decisive action than to simply let this happen. Then, there are also times when the only encouragement you'll receive comes from your own heart and spirit. You must continue to tell yourself what Ida Stewart from Estee' Lauder said in her workshop… "I am, I can and I will." I am not what they think I am. I will be the change they need to see. Being aware of who you are is imperative to be purposeful about your future.

USING POSITIVE SELF-TALK WHEN NETWORKING

Positive self-talk when networking and during business socials builds positive relationships; while negative self-talk causes us to be fearful and even timid when relating to others. Here are some examples of negative and positive self-talk.

Negative:

"Why should anyone want to talk or listen to me? They're all more knowledgeable than I am. After all, I'm the new kid on the block."

"I don't really have anything interesting or intelligent to say; so I had better keep my mouth shut!"

"I've always had problems meeting new people. That's just the way I am. Let me find someone I know to interact with."

"I don't want to say anything stupid and interrupt their flow. No reason to pretend I like being here when I would rather be doing my job."

Positive:

"I know we are all busy women who are under a lot of stress. Maybe I can bring some cheer to the conversation."

"Although I don't know anyone here, this will be a great time to add to my client list and simply get acquainted."

"Because I've been in this position a while, I might be able to make a contribution or share a better approach."

"I bet if I try, I can add a measure of insight to help guide this process along."

"I'm busy, but I can take a minute to share my thoughts."

Positive self-talk will impact your thoughts, behavior and the way you are perceived by others. It's not always their fault when facial expressions change when you arrive. Perhaps it's your approach and negativity that sours the atmosphere. So, let's not blame, but simply attempt to change.

ON THE CORPORATE SIDE

When speaking with mid-level management as a trainer, I learned a great deal about their expectations from a "Needs Assessment" questionnaire. This required a conversation with upper-level management regarding performance and behavior. It included areas such as corporate dress codes, customer service needs or organizational weaknesses.

From these discussions, I learned what qualities and attributes the organization valued in its employees. A number of companies were interested in developing competencies to build interpersonal relationships for women. I found that whether we like it or not, women are often scrutinized more than men regarding their professional demeanor and appearance. For some reason, expectations of "knowing what to do" were many times greater for men than for women. I never read any research on this, but perhaps it's because women are often considered "image makers" and make a real impact on the company's reputation. There is a working definition I generally use when discussing business protocol and etiquette. However, we must first understand the difference between protocol and etiquette.

Nan Leaptrott, author of "Rules of the Game: Global Business Protocol" and President of Global Business Consultants, has been my personal mentor for over 20 years.

She makes this statement about protocol versus etiquette: "Many people use the terms etiquette and protocol interchangeably, but in fact they are different. Protocol is *what to do*. Etiquette is *how to do it*—and how to do it gracefully."

Whether we are speaking about protocol or etiquette, both require a captivating professional presence. Being careful to maintain a sense of class and dignity can belong to every woman. But, first we must know and recognize what is required.

Business and social etiquette know-how is not just for a privileged few with social clout and deep pockets. Every woman who works both in and outside her home, should learn how to diplomatically handle complex business situations, and how to manage business relationships with ease.

The higher we go up on the corporate ladder, the more scrutiny we get. We don't get a pass just because we didn't go to charm school or because our last boss was negligent. Corporate class is competence with a capital "C." You owe it to yourself to get the knowledge required to be your business best. The Bible teaches us that to whom much is given, much is required. When we reach the top, everyone is looking up—for guidance and a good example as well.

LEARNING TO THINK DIFFERENTLY

Much of what I have shared so far represents some of the road markers that transformed my professional life. I learned to think differently about my circumstances and apply new attitudes and behaviors to advance my career.

I have learned that the best way to face shortcomings in one's personal and professional life is to acknowledge weakness and then work hard to improve. Some areas I had to work on were to:

- Meet required deadlines.

- Listen carefully to instructions and follow through.

- Be courteous and respectful to colleagues, clients and guests even when they are rude.

- Meet the required standards of excellence on all projects—not just the ones I enjoyed working on.

Greatness is not the absence of weakness; it is the mastery of weakness.
–Mike Murdock

This quote is a favorite of mine and merits notation because this is where we can linger in limbo feeling sorry for ourselves. Weaknesses can cause us to compare ourselves with others. We even make self-defeating moves; shooting ourselves in the foot by trying to nervously apologize—when indeed, we simply don't have what it takes to get the job done.

There is, however, what I call the "University of Life." With a little time and effort, we all learn how to become better stewards of our gifts and talents. To address areas of weakness we can collect information by reading blogs, listening to podcasts and webinars, as well as, exploring other cultures and communities.

However, information is of no value unless you are willing to change your thinking. No matter how much exposure we get, nothing happens until we learn to think and act differently. This requires putting knowledge into application. Worry does not help either. We get concerned when people reject what we say or believe. This often stops us from advancing. This energy could be better applied by admitting that we're stuck somewhere in the past and determining to blaze a new trail for ourselves and our futures. We simply need to find the code and the key that will unlock our potential.

Thinking differently is a discipline. It's hard work. Sometimes it takes closing our eyes to block out some of the things we actually see and hear. We cannot afford to be blinded by focusing on our weaknesses. Instead we must learn, as Mike Murdock suggests, how to master our perceived weaknesses.

BUSINESS FINESSE

Managing your business professionally requires maintaining standards of excellence and confidentiality. Take note of the following tips to earn the respect you deserve.

Appointments

- Be on time. If you are late, remember to apologize and offer an explanation. Remember not to chew gum in public—especially if you are "on duty" or working in an official capacity. Mints are much better to freshen your breath.

- Be cordial to the secretary, receptionist or person at the front desk when you arrive. Remember they may discuss their impression of you after you leave.

- Present your business card to the receptionist when you arrive for an appointment. Be prepared to offer your business card to a senior executive who asks for it.

- Watch your sitting and standing posture. Sit-up straight with your back against the chair. As a lady, cross your legs at the ankle rather than at the knee and be careful to sit modestly with your knees together when you are wearing a skirt or dress.

- As a guest in an office, don't make yourself too much at home. Put cell phones and electronic devices away and on mute or vibrate. Sit attentively and alert while waiting to see your contact or client. Remember, someone may be observing you even when you don't notice.

- Remember to pick up your feet and walk confidently when moving from one space to another. Body language and facial expressions send powerful messages.

- When you're invited into someone's office space, give a compliment or say something pleasant before you get down to business, i.e., "My, what a nice office you have here."

- Professional courtesy requires that you stand and wait until you've been invited to be seated. Do not walk in and arbitrarily choose a seat. Be sure to watch for a directive as to where you're to sit.

- Respond to questions with confidence and brevity. Pay attention to body language. Avoid slang and do not bore a person by saying too much and talking too long.

- When sitting, always stand to shake hands. It's discourteous to remain seated when approached for a handshake.

- Never reach over a desk to shake hands. When sitting behind a desk, stand and walk around the desk to approach the person before shaking hands.

- Always attempt to begin and end a business conversation on a positive note. Show interest if you're interested and if not, thank the client, sales representative or guest for the opportunity to exchange ideas, goods or services.

- Don't forget to send a thank you email or text in an informal situation or a formal card to express appreciation for awards, citations and other formal recognitions.

PROFESSIONAL EXCELLENCE

Let's explore specific business etiquette and customer service principles to learn how businesses and organizations earn positive and negative ratings. The following statistics reveal how and why particular entities stand out in the marketplace.

First and foremost, it's always important to treat our clients well by offering good customer service. Image professionals know that customer service and business etiquette are intricately connected. Statistics show that:

- Poor service is the No. 1 reason why customers leave and never return. (Small Business Administration)

- The U.S. economy loses over $300 billion a year in lost sales due to poor service. (Gallup)

- Word of mouth referrals are 10 times more effective than advertising campaigns. (Independent Study)

- Customers who have lodged a complaint to an organization and had it satisfactorily resolved tell an average of *five people* about the treatment they received. (ASQCI)

The bottom line is, to stay in business we must go above and beyond to take care of our clients and customers. We must honor our contracts and follow through on our commitments. This way, we enjoy repeat business and earn brand loyalty. Taking care to treat our clients with courtesy and respect is the best way to stand out from our competitors and command the attention we deserve.

THE POWER OF PRESENCE

When walking into a room, which will make the greater impression—what someone says, what they are wearing, or what they do?

Research shows that the first and most important impression we make is related to our business presence... our posture... appearance... and facial expressions. As is true in our social lives, this is reflected in our grooming, clothing and gestures.

For this reason, what the person is wearing and their non-verbal messages are most important. Don't forget... "Silently, we speak the loudest."

Having an appropriate business image in the workplace is profoundly important. People do business with people they know, like and trust. Professional people are looking to do business with other professionals. This means they'll be observing and scrutinizing you before you say a word.

Your business counterparts want to determine whether you are genuine, credible and trustworthy. Although image is important, it will never replace substance and your inherent trustworthiness. Are you a hard worker? Are you ethical and honest?

Failure to hit the mark is never the fault of the target.
To improve your aim, improve yourself.
–Construction Digest

Your willingness to improve and to manage your business image and presence will allow you to step into responsible positions of leadership. Company manuals will often stipulate dress codes and expectations for the workplace. Taking care to follow company protocol in standards of dress shows your willingness to comply as a team player who cares about the credibility and reputation of the organization.

YOUR BUSINESS ATTIRE

Your overall business look should reflect both the business environment you work in, as well as, your position. Being able to adapt—even when your personal preferences are challenged, can be a true test to your ability to adjust. Having the ability and creativity to flow with the signature style of your workplace, yet reflect your own personality and individuality can be challenging.

For instance, the CEO in a pharmaceutical company will project a different image than the sales professional in a shoe manufacturing company. No matter your position or title, commit to excellence in grooming and style.

When gauging what is appropriate in your work environment, take note of others already performing this function. Who do you think does the best job at representing both their position and the company?

Then look at senior level positions—those to whom you will report. How do they dress? Depending upon your position, choose a style that is comfortable for you—and that fits their corporate culture.

Never try to deliberately out-dress those who are in senior positions when you're in junior management or below. Dressing too casually can also hurt your reputation when the company culture is more formal. In most workplace environments, you can find suitable examples to follow and gauge what's appropriate with no problem.

THREE BASIC CLASSIFICATIONS OF BUSINESS-READY ATTIRE

Corporate—This is the most formal style in professional dress. Women who work in law, finance, ministry, television and politics may need to adopt this look. This style of dress conveys a look of authority and the perception of power, which enables others to more readily trust their actions and behavior.

Communicator—This style offers the most comfort for many workers and is business-ready but less formal. Women who work in creative fields such as fashion, education, technology, real estate, advertising, sales, clerical, public relations, marketing and the arts usually have the freedom to dress in a more relaxed manner. Professionals working in these careers will want a more approachable look to encourage friendly interaction with their clients.

Casual—In today's business culture, the casual "dress down" look seems to have taken over the workplace. For this reason, in all three categories of business-ready attire, a creative and more relaxed style has become the norm.

Even for the most formal corporate business environments—many of the rules we once observed have changed. Although wearing a sports jacket or suit coat is often appropriate, we find that popular styles incorporate jeans for business-ready attire.

As you search for what feels right for you, make certain to check standards set by management. Company dress codes vary from industry-to-industry.

SHOPPING FOR COMFY BUSINESS-READY ATTIRE

Shopping for both men and women can cause headaches because we lack the knowledge to do it properly; and we would all like to avoid the wasted dollars often spent on needless items.

Here are some important keys to smart shopping. Ask yourself:

- If I purchase this item, can I dress it up and down?

- Will the color, fabric and style coordinate with other pieces?

- Is it appropriate and does it send the right message?

- Will the style compliment my body type, personality and coloring?

- Will what I'm wearing comply with written dress codes?

- Is what I'm wearing too bright, tight, flashy or revealing? Reserve low and plunging necklines for events after 5 pm.

- Even though going sleeveless at work has become accepted, remember jackets, blazers and sleeves always communicate professionalism.

- If you wear your toes out on a casual day, make sure there are no safety issues and that you're complying with company dress code.

Remember that clothing should skim the shape of the body—not cling to every curve. Men are highly visual. Sexy garments are distracting. If you have to pull and tug; your buttonholes are stretched and your panty lines show—the garment is too tight.

POOR GROOMING GOT-CHA'S

When out running errands, don't grab just any old thing to wear. Although you certainly don't want to look like Ms. Corporate Exec when grocery shopping, you also don't want to run out in wrinkles. When you do, you will invariably run into someone you would like to date!

Looking fresh and fab no matter where you go is always smart. Never be caught with one or more of these:

- Bad breath and no mints

- Chipped nails that are too long for comfort

- Scuffed and worn-down shoes that are soiled

- Crusty heels and ashy skin with no lotion in sight

- Jingling and noisy costume jewelry

- Distracting hair color with too much makeup and perfume

GOING PRO WITH BUSINESS NETWORKING

To network refers to the process of building and sustaining mutually beneficial relationships in the marketplace. Both social and professional relationships can help advance a person in his or her career. For this reason, it is important to maintain integrity in both. Be a person others can rely on and respect. A good name in both arenas is priceless.

When you arrive, look and act like you belong there. Make sure you know the social distancing or rules regarding wearing masks—if there are such policies before you arrive. Also, be sensitive to body language. If you see, "Keep your distance," in a person's eyes, be considerate. Simply nod, and lift you hand to say, "Hi." Following the "mirroring" rule—if everyone is fist-bumping or even bumping elbows, you may do the same, but, never feel compelled. Always do what is comfortable for you. Don't become preoccupied with your cell phone, or find a cozy corner to stand in. Instead, hold your head up, smile and survey the room for a friendly face. Remember, a confident person doesn't look out of place because they don't act like they're out of place. Don't wait for others to approach you. If you don't know who is hosting, take the initiative and move about the room to show yourself friendly, and help others feel at home.

If you are the host or planning to host an event...

- Survey the venue in advance to design a plan for the space. Make certain the room is large enough to accommodate the number of guests expected.

- Make sure there are enough tables and chairs for guests.

- Take note of the lighting and the location of the windows.

- If this is a stand-up event where individuals will only occasionally sit down, plan ahead to position key people in certain areas of the room for clear access to them.

- Have the most important person such as the main guest stand the furthest from the door to keep the line moving and prevent a crowd from forming.

- Limit the mingling time to an hour or an hour-and-a-half.

- If you are planning a training or conversational event, setting up the chairs in a "U" shape works to help members make eye contact. Use theater style and classroom seating for more formal meetings.

- Before the event, clarify why attendees are there. A planning session prior to the event will help in getting certain people together for particular reasons.

- Remind attendees to redirect "shop talk" to keep conversations open and accessible to everyone.

- A good way to redirect undesirable conversation, i.e. politics, is by saying "We certainly can't do that one justice tonight." Or you might say, "That's a conversation in and of itself!"

- Don't forget how important food is to people who are gathering for any and all reasons. Be certain to plan in advance for more than enough coffee, punch, snacks, sandwiches or cookies to arrive at the appropriate time.

THE GIST OF GESTURES

Making a positive first impression includes displaying body language that communicates open, courteous receptivity. Non-verbal language or silent messaging includes flipping your hair, tapping your pencil and frowning. These gestures get noticed as sending either positive or negative messages. Facial expressions are particularly important. You can receive or reject others simply by the way you look at them.

Listed below are common gestures and habits that sometimes send the wrong message. Do you...

- Fold your arms? This can send a message that you are guarded and disengaged. Relax your arms to send a message of openness.

- Slouch? Hold your head up, stand tall and move naturally and easily without dragging your feet. Working on good posture improves your appearance—giving you a look of grace and dignity from head to toe.

- Point when you're speaking? This can leave an impression that you are condescending or scolding. Instead, open your hand and gesture with your palms up—showing that you are anxious to receive information rather than positioning yourself to give orders.

- Look over your glasses as you're observing or speaking? This can cause you to appear patronizing. Adjust your glasses so that they stay on your nose; or pull them up when they slide down and look through the lenses.

- Roll your eyes or look away when speaking to others? Making good eye contact sends the right message. It says I'm engaged, focused and interested in getting to know you or what you're saying.

- Wave your hands while speaking; play with your hair or pop your knuckles? Each of these gestures can be very irritating and annoying, sending a message of nervousness or pre-occupation. Hands are useful tools of communication. Use them intentionally when communicating with others.

- Keep your hands in your pockets while speaking, or jingle keys or change in your pockets? This can send a message that you're uncomfortable or hiding something. Keep your hands visible, using them in a comfortable and non-threatening way as you speak.

KEYS TO CONVERSATION

Do you look approachable when showing up for a networking event or business social? "Mastering the mingling" is a professional skill that allows clients, business partners, and others to connect in a non-threatening and comfortable way.

You may be a mom, educator, an aspiring entrepreneur or an active community leader. You may have a great recipe to share. Conversation starters are as abundant as butterflies in spring. If you will commit to following a few simple guidelines, you will be comfortable at the next networking event.

Remember that, strangers are simply people you haven't met yet. So, don't be afraid to take the lead.

- When you arrive, walk into the room with confidence, purpose and direction.

- Survey the room for a friendly face. Don't wait for others to approach you first. Be willing to approach those with whom you make eye contact and introduce yourself.

- To ease the pain of socializing... and as a matter of politeness, understand that you don't have to do all the talking.

- Informal socials and business gatherings are the perfect opportunity to get to know others outside work.

- Using humor in conversation will help others relax. Stay clear of gossip and off-color jokes.

- People enjoy talking about themselves... Take advantage. Circulating around the room shows an interest in meeting others and builds confidence.

- Ask questions. Encourage those you meet to talk about their professions or families. This is an important communication skill when making business connections.

- Don't get too personal when asking questions, i.e., "How much money did you make when you worked there?" or "Are you married yet?"

- You're a present to the world... let your giftedness shine.

ARTFUL BUSINESS COMMUNICATIONS

The "feminine mystique," as mentioned earlier, is a life infused with courtesy, care and consideration to the degree that it brings a majestic presence to the individual, and powerfully impacts those around them.

For instance, the open palm, facing upward is invitational. It sends a message of openness and the ability to receive from others. This approach is important when speaking publically and in private conversations during networking events.

Several years ago, I created an acronym and a formula for "P.A.L.M." to help individuals with networking skills. During casual conversation, it's important to introduce yourself, then be sensitive to the flow of conversation, and know when to move on and get acquainted with others.

It can be annoying after holding a pleasant conversation to look up and see the person you just spoke with peering over your shoulder. This can happen when colleagues or guests in a group of unfamiliar people get comfortable with you but are hesitant to converse with others.

Circulating around the room helps you overcome unneeded fears. Getting rid of the "clinging vine" syndrome is necessary if you are the person who gets the jitters around people you don't know.

Yes, I get it. Walking around a room of strangers trying to find someone to talk with can be intimidating. However, go ahead... Let the butterflies in your stomach help motivate you to move forward in a positive direction.

Once you shake hands and engage in conversation with one or two people, move on. Don't let fear grip you. Practice the art of exchanging a few conversational pleasantries with one person—then another. It becomes easier each time you do it and the results are rewarding. Let's look at how it's done.

The P.A.L.M. effect is a four-step method for networking engagements:

Positive presence—Introduce yourself with a smile; keep it positive as you engage in conversation. You may even want to exchange information on how to keep in touch.

Ask questions—Show that you are genuinely interested in the other person. Ask about their interests and occupation.

Listen well—No need to do all the talking. We have two ears so do twice the listening.

Move on—Be confident enough to move around the room and introduce yourself to others.

Words are powerful influential tools. Choose them wisely. An inappropriate word can leave the wrong impression with an important business client.

Remember that VIP's have an unspoken manner of behavior when dealing with people at social events. They sometimes arrive on or slightly after the starting hour; they talk little and leave early.

MAKING PROFESSIONAL INTRODUCTIONS

- Introduce a person of business prominence or a high-ranking official to others in your company. Ex: Mr. Baldwin, this is Stanley Shultz, the vice president of sales. Stan, this is Carl Baldwin, the CEO of our company on the West coast."

- When introducing persons in business, age and gender are not considered. Introduce a client or person with a lesser title to those of rank. "Dr. Casey, this is my colleague, Rebecca Lloyd. She is the administrative assistant to my supervisor, Ann Kennedy. Rebecca, this is Dr. Robert Casey. He is the president of Casey Pharmaceuticals."

- Gentlemen should stand to greet a lady. Business introductions require a lady to shake hands when introducing herself.

- If you don't remember a name, make eye contact and say, "I'm sorry. I know we've met before, but I don't remember your name."

- Never shake hands while reaching over a desk or table. Always come around the desk to meet the person face-to-face.

- It is always appropriate for gentlemen to open doors for a lady and to help her with her coat. Although some women in business express the power to manage alone, it's courteous to offer and acceptable if she declines.

Make note of these interesting statistics. It takes...

- Five seconds to make an impression.

- 21 days to start a pattern.

- 100 days for the pattern to become automatic.

- 30 days for a message, without repetition, to be forgotten.

Understand how quickly an impression is made, as well as, how quickly it's forgotten. It's important to stand out from the crowd—not because you made a big scene or wore the most stunning outfit, but because you chose to be warm, inviting and receptive.

Then, after your event is over, say thank you by sending an email or text—especially if you desire to keep in touch.

PROFESSIONAL DINING TIPS

Many times, a networking or business social event involves eating out. Trying to nibble on snacks while drinking a beverage can be awkward and may cause some embarrassment if not handled with finesse.

Have you ever had a person ask your name while your mouth is full? Hmm. What about when a stranger reaches out to shake hands when you know your fingers are wet and salty?

Believe it or not, it is possible to enjoy a snack and shake hands as well. This maneuver allows you to hold your food and beverage in your left hand while having your right hand free to shake hands. Here's how:

- Don't fill your plate to overflowing with chips and dip spilling over the sides. Remember—this isn't the last supper. Most often you can return for refills.

- Place your snack plate between the middle fingers of your left hand with sauces and dips placed handily on the side of your plate.

- Hold your beverage on the plate with your forefinger and thumb.

Holding your plate and cup in your left hand, while securing your napkin with your pinky finger underneath your snack plate is the perfect way to circulate around the room; leaving your right hand free to shake hands. Practice this technique—it works. Remember that practice makes perfect.

SIT-DOWN EVENTS

Networking with business colleagues can sometimes include a sit-down event or an occasion such as breakfast, lunch, an outdoor event, or any special time when food is served. These gatherings include:

Dinner Parties or Receptions: A social gathering specifically designed for celebration, networking in business, or recognizing an occasion or milestone such as a retirement or job promotion.

Buffet: An informal meal served on a table or "food bar" where invited guests serve themselves from prepared menu items.

A professional person engages in business matters with a sense of urgency and responsibility. You may find yourself spending a great deal of time negotiating business around a meal. For this reason, some foods should be avoided when you have an important breakfast, lunch or dinner scheduled.

For example, trying to manage a hero sandwich with dripping mustard and sliding tomatoes, onions and pickles can ruin a potential business deal or a job interview. Instead choose menu items that are easily managed with a knife and fork.

As Brillat-Savaarin, the nineteenth-century French gastronome wrote:

> *"The table establishes a kind of bond between the bargainer and the bargained-with, and renders the guest more apt to receive certain impressions."*

RESTAURANT DINING

Make reservations in advance when meeting for business, especially when entertaining several guests. This will help you secure the desired table and minimize your wait time.

- When you make a reservation be on time. You should be no more than 15 minutes late without notifying the restaurant of your tardiness. If you're meeting another party be sure the host or hostess knows.

- If you need to cancel your reservation, call at least a few hours in advance so that they have time to fill the spot.

- Allow your guest to walk ahead of you when escorted to your table.

- A gentleman will lead the way into a restaurant for a lady and will seat her before he is seated.

- Guests of honor—those celebrating a special occasion, i.e., a retirement, a visiting foreign dignitary, a customer or guest with military or government rank, elderly guest, guest with distinguished title or career should be seated to the right of the host.

- The "power" seat or best seat faces the room and should be reserved for the honored guest. The host or co-host is seated at the opposite ends of the table.

- Never seat a guest facing a wall. Also, if there is sunlight brightly shining through a window, the host or hostess should be aware and change seats.

- Never seat your guest near a busy entranceway, near the kitchen, or a busy walk thru. If the waitress or waiter directs the party to such an area, the host can graciously request a more appropriate table location.

- A host helps the lady seated to his right. Once the ladies are seated, the men can be seated.

- To seat a lady, the gentleman should pull out her chair, holding onto the back of it as she seats herself. No need to push or shove. Allow her to guide the process.

- It is good for the host to remember that guests should be invited to sit where each person feels most comfortable for conversation.

- Purses, portfolios, tablets, cell phones and electronic devices should not be placed on the dining table, but kept in your lap, securely hung on a chair, placed in an empty seat or left on the floor.

- Although ladies often choose to sit with their spouses, it's acceptable to sit elsewhere to provide opportunities to get acquainted with others.

DINING ETIQUETTE

- A host should ensure that dinner is served within 20 to 25 minutes after arrival.

- After the guests are seated, the host should order last.

- If wine is being served, allow your guest to select their preferred entrées so that you'll know whether to order red or white wine.

- If you are having a meal with a higher ranked person, client or guest, allow them to initiate the business discussion.

- The host is responsible for keeping conversation going... keep it light and pleasant.

- Never order more than one alcoholic drink at a business meal and two at the most. If you are the host and you don't drink, it is considerate to offer your guest a drink if you know they would like one.

- Order red wine for red meats and white wine for fish, pasta and chicken.

- When eating soup, don't blow or slurp it. Never leave your spoon in the bowl between bites. Sip from the side of the spoon and allow your spoon to rest on the serving plate between bites. Always spoon away from you rather than toward you to avoid a possible splash on your clothing.

- When a lady needs to be excused for the restroom; she only needs to say, "Excuse me, please" or "May I be excused." If she is being accompanied by a gentleman, he should make a gesture to help her with her seat as she stands to leave.

- Select only items from the menu that are easy to eat, especially if you are being interviewed or need to be extra careful about the impression you are making. Save oversized sandwiches, spaghetti, corn on the cob and spareribs for dining alone or with friends.

- If you are being interviewed or another individual is paying for your meal, be considerate by asking, "Have you eaten here before? What do you suggest?" If they say, "The soup and salad is good," take a cue. Don't order from the steak menu. Perhaps their budget requires a less expensive meal.

- Never leave your spoon in a coffee or teacup after stirring. Leave your stirring spoon on your saucer or cup.

- If food gets stuck in your teeth, do not use a toothpick at the table or in public. Flossing your teeth, putting on lipstick and taking medicine should be reserved for the bathroom.

- It is impolite to remove your jacket or loosen your tie unless invited to do so.

- If you bite down on gristle, bone, or a pit, don't call attention to it. Remove it with your fork or fingers and place it on the side of your plate or in a napkin.

- Never wave your utensils while eating and talking, or drink from a cup or glass with one hand while holding a fork or spoon with another.

- If you drop a utensil on the floor, simply notify the waiter or waitress and ask for a replacement. The same is true with your napkin. Never search for it during the meal.

- Be certain to leave utensils in a "4:20" position after completing your meal. The fork is placed underneath the knife and the spoon under the fork on the upper right rim of your plate.

- Both during and after a meal, use your napkin to wipe away crumbs. When finished, the napkin is placed to the left of your plate... unfolded and slightly crumpled.

ORDERING SUBSTITUTES

- When asking for a substitute, a polite person will select one of the offered substitute or side items. But, if nothing seems appealing, ask your server if there are other items you didn't notice on the menu.

- If the substitution is not allowed, the waiter will often try to work out something. Please don't insist on having it your way. It's never appropriate to make a scene for any reason in a public place.

- If they cannot allow a substitution, recognize that it's likely the policy of the manager or restaurant due to the extra cost. You can either offer to pay extra for the side item or order something else. Remember, waiters are only doing their job; they are not the decision makers.

- Sending a dish back because it's the wrong order, overcooked or undercooked always tends to be awkward. But this is not considered bad manners if done politely, especially if it's not cooked precisely the way you requested.

- If you're entertaining a guest, make certain they are happy with their order. It may seem rude or send the wrong message if they're not happy and you ignore their dissatisfaction.

Accidents and mistakes do happen, so make certain you are polite when you tell your server about the mistake. Don't forget to thank them for correcting it.

A TIMELY TIP

Tipping is important when it comes to discussing restaurant etiquette.

- Since servers typically make less than minimum wage, they depend on tips to make extra money. If you are satisfied with your service, a standard tip is no less than 15-20 percent.

- If the server was exceptional, you can leave more. Similarly, you can leave a smaller tip if you were displeased with the service. However, let your server know if you are dissatisfied so that they do not merely assume you forgot to leave them the standard amount.

- Don't forget to leave your tip with a thank you, a smile and hopefully a genuine compliment that will make the person feel that he or she has encountered an exceptional individual.

HANDLING AWKWARD FOODS

Some foods are awkward and do not facilitate dining with comfort and ease. When in doubt, always use your knife and fork... not your fingers. When you know what to do and how to do it, you can dine with comfort and ease.

Hors d' Oeuvres—Do not dip your finger foods or chips into sauces or dips that are in a serving bowl. Use a spoon (hopefully a serving spoon is provided) to place the sauces or dip on your plate. You can then dip until your heart is content.

Pasta—Use your fork to twirl a few strands by placing the tines against the plate while twirling, or you can use a spoon in the left hand (if you are right-handed) to use as a "stopper" as you twirl. Never slurp or suck spaghetti in your mouth. Use a fork to cut your pasta.

Soup—When eating soup, place your spoon in the front side of the bowl, and scoop it away from you. Do not drink from your bowl. You may tilt the bowl away from you to get the last few bites. Do not slurp; sip quietly from the side of the spoon... the whole spoon should not go in the mouth. Finally, rest the spoon on the saucer or plate underneath the bowl between bites.

Salads—Some salads have chunks and pieces that are too large to easily bite. Use your knife to cut into bite-size pieces. Cherry tomatoes, if bite-size can be eaten whole. If they are extra-large, they should be carefully cut in half with a knife. Never nibble from large pieces that are on your fork.

Bacon, Sausage or French fries—All are considered finger foods if they are crisp. If not, you may use a fork and knife to cut them into bite-size pieces.

Fruit and cheese—Cut fresh fruit and soft cheese with a knife and fork. Hard cheese is often served as a finger food.

Baked/fried chicken—Always use a knife and fork to cut meat or chicken unless you are at a picnic or outdoor event. If your host or hostess picks up their chicken to eat with their fingers, you may choose to do so also... or use your knife which is also appropriate.

Jumbo shrimp—If at a party, you may use your fingers to munch and dip. Use a dinner or fish knife to cut and dip if you are attending a formal event.

Sorbet—This is usually considered a dessert and can be eaten with a spoon. When served as a palate cleanser, it is eaten with a dessert fork.

TOASTING SPECIAL GUESTS

Offering a toast is a common gesture at special events such as weddings and other formal events. A toast is a salute or a verbal recognition of an individual's accomplishments. This gesture is intended to honor a special guest. At times, the toast is given in recognition of a milestone, such as a retirement, or can be for someone with whom the company wants to do business. Keep the following in mind when giving a toast:

- Guests should have a beverage, wine or champagne in their glasses.

- The person being honored should not stand or raise his or her glass for the toast. They should remain seated and allow others to drink to them. They should nod in appreciation and follow with a sip.

- The host or person giving the toast will stand, but the guests are not required to do so unless the guest of honor is from a foreign company, judge, ambassador or a very elderly distinguished person.

- When toasting, raise your glass and make eye contact with the person being honored if they are seated at your table, or look in their direction and nod your head before sipping.

- It is also nice to turn to each of your dinner guests, raising your glass, nodding and then sipping.

- Ensure waiters and waitresses are aware of your expectations so that the room is quiet with no walking around. The best time is usually after dessert has been served when everyone has a beverage available.

- The person chosen to give the toast should be well-spoken and able to make flattering and appropriate comments. The toast should be short, light and brief—about one minute and no longer than three.

- The host of the event has the first opportunity to honor the special guest. If it looks as though a toast will not be offered, a senior member of the organization can whisper to the host, "Would you mind if I raise a toast?" Most often, the request would be granted.

- Never tell off-color jokes or share an embarrassing incident during a toast. Never belittle the guest of honor in any way.

- As the guest of honor, try to respond immediately to a toast from your host or anyone else.

- Thank your host or the person who toasted you by saying something pleasant like, "Thank you, Sharon, for your kind words of welcome. And, Larry, you have provided an excellent meal. It's wonderful to be with you and your delightful staff again in New York. You've made me feel very special tonight."

- If you, as the honoree or special guest would like to informally toast your host at a restaurant, simply raise your glass to your host and say something like this, "Clara, I am really grateful for the retirement luncheon you organized for me today. This is a day I will never forget. Thank you."

- If someone raises a toast and you have nothing left in your glass to drink, lift your glass as a gesture and pretend to drink. It is also acceptable to raise your water glass.

Civility costs nothing and buys everything.
–Lady Mary Wortley Montagu

BUSINESS SOCIAL FAUX PAS

The following behaviors can damage a professional career or reputation:

- Drinking too much—more than one or two cocktails or alcoholic beverages.

- Showing improper behavior, i.e., flirting, talking loudly, gossiping or revealing confidential information.

- Dressing inappropriately or in a revealing manner.

- Behaving as though you're attending a social event with friends.

- Exhibiting poor or sloppy dining etiquette... this applies to the buffet table and hors d'oeuvres.

- Treating the host, guests or servers rudely or dismissively.

- Telling off-color or tasteless jokes or stories.

- Failing to tip persons at the bar, coat check, valet or chauffeur.

- Arriving with or leaving the event with the wrong person. Allow others to use their own transportation to avoid rumors.

- Failing to thank your manager and party organizer before departing and again the next business day.

TECH ETIQUETTE

From phone calls to text messaging, technology has given us countless ways to connect with one another. The question is—what form of communication is appropriate, and at what time?

- Text messaging: "Texting is a brief transmission of facts," i.e. appointments, notifications, sending contact info, etc. The risk in text-based messaging is the loss of tone or context. If you are concerned that the message will be misinterpreted, make a phone call. Texting on the job can be controversial and seen as unprofessional. For this reason, I would advise against it, unless you are conducting business on a company cell phone. Social media sites: Generally speaking, Facebook is used for establishing personal connections while LinkedIn is for business networking. It is safe to stay off social media sites during work hours, unless it's part of your work assignment. Remember to put privacy settings on your social media accounts to keep your personal life private.

- Email: It is impolite to totally ignore a message whether personal or professional. People expect an immediate or same-day response—or at least within 24 hours. If you know there will be a delay, respond by indicating receipt of the message and state when a reply can be expected. If the message has weighty implications, always stop and reflect before hitting "send."

- Use of your mobile phone: Be self-aware of your surroundings when speaking on your mobile device. Be careful not to yell or speak loudly within earshot of others. Understand that phone technology allows the voice to be transmitted at a normal or low volume.

- Never use your mobile device:

  - While driving or when in a checkout line, as it slows the process down for everyone.

  - During a class or training. This is inconsiderate and can be disruptive to the professor or speaker.

- During a religious service or ceremony, i.e., wedding, funeral, etc.

- While with clients at work. If you are being paid to do a job, your cell phone should be off. Your attention should be with your client or on your assignment.

- When you are with family and friends and/or dining in a nice restaurant. Facetime is essential to building healthy relationships. Don't miss out on real life to interact with someone virtually.

- During public events such as movies, plays and concerts.

UNIVERSAL ETIQUETTE

We should never underestimate the importance of "business presence," which includes exemplary manners and a work ethic that warrants a promotion. This is business class at its best.

Operating with excellence means business etiquette rules begin with the CEO and flow from there to upper and middle management... to the receptionist.

My mentor and friend wrote, "Rules of the Game: Global Business Protocol" to bring cultural and social awareness to the workplace and to classrooms. We all get along better when we understand one another. Her book is a must read for anyone with global aspirations in the marketplace. She wrote:

- Keep your hands to yourself, off yourself and out of your pockets.

- Don't point... Gesture with your full hand, not your fingers.

- Respect age—especially when speaking to seniors, err on the side of formality.

- Dress conservatively. Be clean and neat.

- Don't use given names unless invited to.

- Reciprocate hospitality when it is possible.

- Don't tell jokes or attempt humor when you don't know the guests.

- Be punctual in business, even if others are not—don't show annoyance at being kept waiting.

- At a meal, wait for your host to start. Don't discuss politics, crime, religion or personal topics.

Companies that pride themselves in building strong client relationships must be invested in the principles of business etiquette. Although this topic cannot be fully exhausted here, it's good to know that with some basic professional keys to excellence, we can make a lasting ripple effect that will impact a multitude. As representatives of God's kingdom, we can't afford to be anything less than our very best.

CHAPTER SIX

FASHION FINESSE

O N A RECENT trip to White House Black Market for a Mother's Day ensemble, I came across a unique tag. It was attached to a blouse and had the word "ICONIC" imprinted on it with a shiny, crystal-like heart that instantly caught my attention. On the reverse side was a message in bold white lettering against a black background.

It read: "Today I'm long pearls, big glasses and shiny patent. Today I'm flawless. Today I'm flirty. Today I'm an icon. WHBM.com." The word "icon" means image. Thus, "iconic" means larger than life, enormous, gargantuan and impressive. Without question, this brand is intentional about its message and is certain to get noticed. The question now is, will your brand name do the same for God?

What message are you sending to your audience today? As a representative of the kingdom—realm and domain of God—what does your tag of authenticity say? If you are a mom, does your attitude and appearance convey competence and sincerity about your responsibilities? If you own a company, when you step into the room, does your posture, the words you speak offer a positive and confident presence?

You are a total package composed of personality traits, attitudes, gestures—and your appearance speaks volumes. Your tagline is a messenger communicating to the space you occupy. What are you wearing today? Does your look express the iconic person you were meant to be—drawing others to you—or do you convey uncertainty and self-doubt repelling those around you?

Every woman is a unique "gift package" that distinguishes her from other women. This unique package reveals an iconic brand that will clearly resonate with those looking for a special gift or talent. Your stylistic look will either attract or detract. You must decide on how you present yourself to others—understanding that your look will attract a certain kind of person.

Because we are busy taking cues from others about what to wear or what's *not* attractive, we fail to evaluate our own special taste in dress and style—or the uniqueness of our eyes or shapely figure. Perhaps you have hair that could be featured on a Pantene commercial. Your "package" includes all the wonderful qualities that compose your looks, personality and ability to attract others to you.

Iconic brands make their statement in an unapologetic way because they mean business… and they understand that no attention means no business! Their boutique can stock exotic clothing and unique accessories from all around the world… But if no one notices, or is attracted to what they offer, they will quickly go out-of-business. They want the world to know that they are serious. Ask yourself about your own significance. How serious are you about offering the gifts, talents, and qualities you possess in an attractive way?

We receive approximately 80-90 percent of our information through our eyes, which makes us visual creatures. For this reason alone, we should realize that what appeals to our sense of sight, heavily impacts our attitudes and actions.

Take a moment to think about what grabs your attention. When you are out-and-about, what catches your eye about a person's style and appearance? Notice what you like or perhaps don't like. If you like what you see, consider how you might design the look, but with your own creative spin.

Be so good that they can't ignore you.
–Steve Martin

As an image professional, I know that the first order of business for sales professionals is to get their client's attention. Not only do they want to get their visual attention, but they want to engage as many senses as possible. WHBM brand wants to get you into its stores to see the colors, feel the fabric and enjoy their legendary customer service. Sounds almost silly but they captured my attention and drew me in with that catchy clothing tag.

FINDING YOUR OWN ICONIC BRAND MARKER

Have you been in hiding simply because you aren't really sure what looks good on you? Hide no more. It's time to discover your iconic brand marker. A marker is a distinguishing identifier. It is a symbol of distinction. We see many symbols on our shoes and handbags. When we see Michael Kors,

Dooney & Bourke, Coach, or Chanel, we think luxury and the world's most influential brands.

Shoes and handbags from Walmart simply do not carry the same cachet. Why? Because that name represents an economy brands. However, we can choose to upgrade our look at a specialty store like T.J. Maxx without spending much more money. This means we never have to settle for less. Affordability can even be found at Nordstrom, which is known for carrying prestigious brands. In other words, you can learn to be a savvy shopper by looking for sales and value buys at countless stores.

What do people think when they see you? Is it apparent that you have put some thought and time into your appearance? What value does your "brand name" carry? Does your look convey value, or do you look a bit outdated and out of touch?

Remember that polyester and silk carry two very different messages. The fabrics we wear, and the care we take to present our best, speak loudly regarding the value we place on our talents and image. As I mentioned earlier, beauty is not about facial features, body measurements or how much we spend. It's simply about caring enough to invest the time and energy to present our very best.

There is no greater treasure on earth than you. If someone put a $500 check in your pocket without your knowledge, you couldn't spend it because you wouldn't know it was there. Likewise, the value of your talent or voice will never be seen or heard unless you decide to showcase it in a special way.

As I mentioned before, White House Black Market is a "get noticed" stand out brand for me. Because of the COVID pandemic, many iconic brands won't survive. However, women's boutiques that last, provide its valued customers and clients with an atmosphere of quality, elegance and excellence. Most of the fashion pieces are strikingly black and white with splashes of accent colors.

The WHBM store also has many accessories to choose from, including shoes, belts, handbags, jewelry and scarves. I feel that my look communicates excellence in taste and dress when I am wearing my new ensemble—so I will be back to shop again—either online or at a boutique. Do I sound like a commercial? … Of course I do. If you like a garment, you'll promote it either verbally or visually, simply because looking great helps you feel great.

It's time for you to be your own kind of beautiful! "Get Noticed!" is all about helping you create your own distinctive brand. Let's peel the onion back and see what's revealed. Stand out brands:

- Make positive powerful first impressions.

- Make visual statements that communicate excellence.

- Deliver what they promise making them reputable and memorable.

- Are marked by high standards of quality that encourage trusting and lasting relationships.

The bottom line is… distinctive brands "get noticed!" And now it's time to identify your unique or iconic brand marker—more commonly known as your "signature look." You will identify your fashion personality, the colors that are right for you, your figure type and more.

Remember, your gifts and talents are unique, original and significant. The more you know about your "gift package," and learn to value and appreciate your distinct qualities, the more others will appreciate and benefit from them.

I haven't always known or understood what looks good on me or how to express my individuality. Too often I focused on comparing myself with others. Now, I know who I am, what I like, and I'm very precise and selective when I dress. You can be too.

Remember, style isn't something that you stumble into… It takes work! If you care to expend the time and energy, you can easily define the look that compliments your body type, and makes you feel comfortable and look great. You don't need the budget of a celebrity to look like one. Because I have invested time, practice and skill into the art of image consulting, I'm now confident with my personal look and can help others.

I have many testimonials from women. One of them went like this: "The best decision I ever made with my jumbled up closet was to hire someone to come to my house and go through my closet piece-by-piece. I knew I needed to update my look. My consultant showed me combinations of items from my closet that would work well together and helped me get rid of those that no longer served me. After that came an appointment to an upscale store. When we were done, I felt like a celebrity! It was worth every penny."

I believe this chapter will help you upgrade your wardrobe and self–esteem. Here, you will learn to:

- Apply image techniques to enhance your physical assets, while camouflaging figure challenges.

- Improve your appearance by becoming self-aware of your body type and wardrobe personality.

- Apply principles of color and investment dressing to update your wardrobe, while stretching your clothing dollar.

- Become an expert on stylizing your custom look for affordability and comfort.

I realize some women don't care to invest the time or energy to focus on style, color and trends. They prefer minimal to no makeup with a simple free-style look. Of course, there is nothing wrong with going free and easy;

however, I think it's important to always keep a few fundamentals in mind so you'll always appear well groomed.

Here are some tips and keys… even if you aren't particularly hooked on fashion:

- Watch current fashion trends so you don't appear outdated.

- Clean out your closet at the end of warm and cold seasons. Get rid of items that are tired, no longer fit, or are outdated.

- Take an inventory of your closet, make a list of color and styles needed before shopping to avoid impulse buying.

- Organize and arrange clothes, hanging like-things together. Do a seasonal inventory to get rid of clutter.
- Be aware when your lifestyle has changed from sporty to business or business to mommy- mode, etc., making sure your wardrobe reflects those life transitions.

People who dislike walking from aisle-to-aisle in a department store looking for the perfect outfit—may find meaning in the statement below:

Style isn't what you wear, it's who you are!
–Kristen Mellette

You've often heard people say, "she's got style" or "she's a classy lady." These are wonderful compliments. A stylish and classy lady has not only made an investment of time and money into what she is wearing, but, has put considerable thought as well. To top this off, her winning personality is obviously shining through.

You won't find these qualities "readymade" on a shelf or a rack. Style is like looking at a complicated puzzle pieces that need to be assembled. The completed work is a masterpiece that requires skill and expertise. That's why professionals are often called to the rescue. Fortunately, you will be blessed to have much of this expertise detailed right here.

WHY HIRE AN IMAGE PROFESSIONAL?

Both men and women hire image professionals or a fashion consultant to help them maximize their signature look. They are looking for an expert to provide an objective opinion. They know that a true professional will assess their personality, body type and profession to analyze their wardrobe, color preferences and more. When you hire a professional you aren't looking for an opinion or an educated guess. You want someone with time-invested-expertise to help you arrive at your desired results.

"Style" can be perplexing; however, every woman can have a stylish classy look if they are willing to make the necessary adjustments. Image professionals specialize in a variety of areas. Some specialize in international protocol and diplomatic services; others prefer to work with those in politics. Some manage the public image of spiritual leaders, television personalities, models, entertainers, musicians and actors. Their services vary depending on the individual or career. This may include:

- Wardrobe and closet inventories and organizing services

- Personal shopping—figure and personality typing, accessorizing services

- Color analysis to include personality and figure typing

- Skin care and makeup services

- Business, social and dining etiquette

- Speaking and coaching, personal and professional development training

- Wedding, entertaining and special event planning and coordination

Professional image services help clients save time, energy and money, however, by reading the following pages, you will have a wealth of information at hand.

EIGHT INSIDER SECRETS TO A FABULOUS NEW YOU

Taking an honest look at yourself is the first step to transformation. Are you petite with a pixie haircut? Do you enjoy outdoor sports and camping? Are you tall and voluptuous with a bold personality—or are you an introvert who enjoys reading and writing? What about your career? Your career and lifestyle will make a difference in choosing the look that is right for you.

Now, let's look at eight insider secrets—strategies used universally by professional stylist to turn drab into fab!

SECRET #1: Perception Is Everything

You may recall the examples I shared earlier about being perceived as a celebrity and the time someone told me that I "looked stunning?" Both times I was simply minding my business, not intending to make an impression. Yet, someone noticed because "perception is everything." We don't live in a vacuum… someone is almost always watching and observing our actions and words.

So, instead of fearing the possibility that someone may glance our way at the wrong time, we must be prepared, realizing that at any time a promotion, job opportunity, or a lifetime partner could be waiting in the wings.

We may be at the supermarket or test driving a new car. Who knows when a life-changing encounter or moment will come?

Dealing with Misperceptions

I once had a client who was challenged on her job, which she believed was related to her size and height. She was a statuesque woman with a pleasing personality, who was in middle-management with a male supervisor.

She explained that whenever she stepped into his office, her boss seemed extremely defensive and uncomfortable. Unpleasant meetings with him were becoming more frequent. She said on many occasions her boss would "cut her down to size" in front of others.

After further discussion, we concluded that my client was dealing with a "perception" issue. Her boss, who stood five-foot-six-inches-tall, was probably intimidated by her six-foot frame. Perhaps his own insecurities caused the issue. She hadn't thought of that.

I began advising her on professional wardrobe techniques to make her appear shorter, and colors that would soften her height and presence. We also strategized about body language and verbal ques.

Our plan was to break the color line when wearing a jacket and skirt or slacks; this would make her look shorter in appearance and less intimidating. I explained that wearing a matching jacket, skirt or slacks creates a visual, vertical line, making a person appear taller. Months later she came to my office with a big smile and a hug. To her amazement, the manager began complimenting her new look. She even received a promotion.

Just as I thought, her boss perceived my client as overbearing because of a misperception. This is not uncommon. Feeling intimidated because of height, gender, race or status, is very real. If anyone feels disqualified from the game, conflict can result. Something or someone must change.

My client also followed through by being less opinionated, and more attentive when listening. This all worked out in her favor. When she became more approachable, her manager became less confrontational. As a result, he perceived her as bringing value to the company and gave her a raise.

SELF-PERCEPTION

The way we perceive ourselves and others will be reflected in our behavior. One key thing I learned in modeling school is the impact of one's self-perception on confidence and behavior. When I enrolled in Roland's International School for Modeling in Fayetteville, NC, I had to face the mirror almost daily. To my surprise, I found this to be intimidating. There was a lot about my appearance that I did not like.

The mirror test revealed the real truth about me. The mirrors that I faced almost every day in the classroom, at first, caused me much discomfort. It took months for me to look full-face in the mirror with a smile of acceptance. I came to realize that mirrors are my friends. Think about it. They don't lie. We simply need to be bold and brave enough to see ourselves as other do.

Let me interject something I learned while in training. There's an art to purchasing mirrors. Make sure the mirror you use every day, isn't a decorative one designed to make rooms look larger because they'll do the same to your waist, stomach, and hips! Mirrors show us everything. And frankly speaking, if there's something in your appearance that isn't appealing or flattering, wouldn't you want to be the first to know? Being clueless may cost your job, a promotion or even discourage a potential life partner.

Hiding never works. By the end of this book, you'll want to embrace your mirror like it's your best friend because essentially... it is your truest fashion friend and shows what we often choose to ignore or are afraid to admit.

One thing I discovered while "looking in the mirror" was my love for sequins and sparkles. Here's the funny thing... even after advising others to create balance and variety in their wardrobes, I repeated a look that was obviously making an over exaggerated fashion statement for me! It goes to prove that we can be blind to our own fashion proclivities and I'm no exception. It's important to remember that we can easily get stuck in a rut if we're not careful. That's why we need image consultants and professional advisors to help us make the best choices.

As we age, our faces and features change. I've had clients tell me they turned their mirrors around, or covered them, to avoid taking a good hard look for fear of seeing gray hair or another wrinkle. Weight gain can cause the same reaction. No matter what, wearing a confident expression helps us value our inner qualities and that brings out the radiance of our giftedness. A smile with a look of confidence is a gift that keeps on giving.

SECRET #2: Embrace Areas You Cannot Change

Take an honest look at your posture, eyes, face, hair, the color of your skin and your body type. No hype and no lies. The truth is there. Do you like what you see?

When you ask this question, two things will be obvious:

1) You will see what you don't like, yet cannot change.

2) You will also see what you can change about your appearance with intentional effort.

Once you make this discovery, you must make a mental commitment to take the necessary steps to reach the desired results.

Action may not always bring happiness;
but there is no happiness without action.
–Disraeli

When I was a teenager, my brother said I looked like an ironing board when I turned to the side. Although I wasn't permanently scarred by this remark, I had to take another look in the mirror. From this statement made in jest, I saw that I wasn't endowed with as much backside cushioning as some of my peers. My challenge was to accept that truth rather than feeling self-conscious about my body. Furthermore, I could not change the physical characteristics of my body structure, which were inherited from my father.

I realized later in life that accepting undesirable facets of your appearance, creates a desire to learn techniques to help you meet those challenges. Throughout the years, I have gained and lost weight. However, there is one thing I recognize about my genetic characteristics–my flat derriere and thin legs will not be going away.

Instead of being ill-at-ease, I've chosen to embrace and embellish my body parts—all of them—slim legs, tiny wrists, short waist and curvy hips—as distinctively beautiful. I often bring up my figure flaws to help my clients become more honest about theirs.

Remember, we are not alone in having a few challenging areas to deal with. Decide to tackle areas of frustration before they get the best of us. As you embrace and love your flaws as well as your more attractive assets, you will walk with confidence, professionalism, and poise. You'll look and feel like royalty!

SECRET #3: Understand the Impact of Color

Color enhances our personal image and is important when choosing cosmetics and clothing. Conscientious meticulous women are curious to know what colors are flattering—and which ones cause them to look lifeless and drab.

The study of color theory shows you what colors compliment your skin tone, hair and eyes, and helps you select the most flattering clothing, accessories, and makeup. Color adds a sense of vibrancy to a person's wardrobe, transforming an ordinary look into an extraordinary one.

So, don't be afraid of color. Add the colors you like to your home and office. The colors most complimentary to you can be used to enhance and upgrade your surroundings as well, giving you a feeling of comfort at work or play.

Definitions: Color Theory and Color Analysis

Color Theory is an intricate scientific system designed to reveal the visual effects of color that are seen in nature, art, culture and fashion. Here we see how color attracts attention, sets a mood or makes a bold and bright statement.

Color analysis involves using clear or blue light to detect undertones in someone's' skin. In the process, color fabric swatches are placed around the neck and face to determine which ones are most complimentary. Professionals such as Color Analysts and Personal Shoppers offer this service to help clients enhance their appearance.

I use the seasonal color system that evaluates an individual's natural coloring; including skin undertones, hair and eye color. Just as we know the characteristics of the four seasons—Winter, Spring, Summer and Autumn, this color system draws a correlation between nature and the undertones found in a person's natural coloring. Certain colors are considered complimentary, while others are not.

Color Me Warm or Color Me Cool

Determining your undertone is foundational to identify your color category. This is defined as the color underneath the surface of the skin. Undertones in one's skin can be seen outdoors in clear light or in a manufactured setting using a blue light.

To describe this process, think of the contrast between the colors of the sun or fire (warm), and water or snow (cool). Now, envision a painting with a burning sun over the ocean. The cool colors of the sky and water tend to recede, or take a back seat to the burning heat of the scorching sun. The dominant presence of the sun will cause it to "stand out" or "advance" on the canvas. This is what warm and cool looks like in harmony.

This concept is also true with colors we wear on our faces and bodies. Crimson red lipstick will stand out boldly on our faces while our blue or gray eye shadow often shows only a hint of color; or our orange scarf provides a bold accent to a brown suit. Here is a brief explanation of the impact of color.

The cool side of color...

- WINTER—The skin tone characteristic of "Winter" is a dominant cool pink/rose undertone. The skin may appear almost white in Caucasian and fair-skin ethnic groups. Asian, African, African-American and other fair-to-dark-skin ethnic groups are oftentimes in the "cool winter" category. Some Asians with an olive-toned or dark-brown complexion look great in winter colors. The eye color is often dark-brown and deep dark-brown. The hair color is medium-to-dark brown, blue-black and black. Winter skin types look great in cranberry reds, royal blues, navy, charcoal-gray, black and white. Stay away from tan, browns and orange.

- SUMMER— The dominant skin tone characteristic of "Summer" is a pale skin color with a rosy-red or pink-lilac undertone. The overall look of this skin tone is almost colorless with a translucent complexion. The hair and eyes can be a silver-blonde, ash-brown to medium-brown. All ethnic and multiracial groups can fall into the summer category. However, most are fair-skin with cool undertones and blue or gray flecks in the eyes. You will want to choose pastels and soft neutrals with rose and blue undertones. Lavender, taupe, powder-pink and powder-blue are complimentary colors. White is your complimentary "neutral" color. Stay away from tan, orange and brown.

The warm side of color...

- SPRING—The dominant skin undertone characteristic of "Spring" is a light amber, tan or yellow-gold undertones. This person has warm undertones that reflect the glow of natural radiance. Their eyes may have yellow or gold flecks, and the hair may be a golden-blonde, strawberry-blonde or light-brown. Complimentary color choices include camel, peach, light-yellow and golden-brown. Avoid dark cool colors like deep purple, raspberry-reds and black which may drain color from your face and make you appear tired and sallow.

- AUTUMN/FALL—The dominant skin undertone characteristic of "Autumn" is a deep gold or deep tan with yellow-gold undertones. Sometimes the skin coloring has an orange-toned coloring with a bronzed look. Some have a deep brown or chocolate-brown eye color with gold or light brown flecks. The hair can be dark brown, auburn or a variety of reds. As with the other seasons of color, all races and ethnic groups can be found in this seasonal color group. Color choices that are complimentary to this type are tan, gold and brown. In addition, camel, beige, orange, and dark brown are favorites. Avoid pure white, blue, pink and gray.

Your knowledge of color will help you in the next step—refining your image and colors to choose when shopping. Which of the categories mentioned are true to your skin tone and coloring?

Then take a look at your makeup collection. Have you selected the right colors for your eyes, lips and face? Now assess your wardrobe. We tend to gravitate toward clothes that feel right. Often, if your undertones are cool, a brown shirt and orange scarf will feel odd against your skin. Carefully evaluate patterns of colors you own, wear, and receive compliments on. This will help you make the right choices for your makeup and clothes.

What's In Your Closet?

Are the colors right for you? Do the clothes fit or are you keeping them in hopes that you will lose or gain weight so you can wear them again? Are you the type to buy the same thing over again, just in different colors because you hate to shop? Or are all your pieces so different that you have difficulty putting appropriate looks together?

Although current trends... and I emphasize the word "trends," allow us to put warms and cools together without a thought, trust me—a look of chaos is on the rise and the message is clear—no thought, rhyme nor reason... Just do it! Whether it's untied shoelaces, unbuckled shoes or holes in jeans and shirts—it all sends a message of disorder. It's an "in your face" theme that is often reflected in behavior and the chaos we see in culture and society.

The anything goes theory with multicolor stripes and prints, and T-shirts and boots with after-five wear will soon give way to something else bizarre. It's ok... it's all fashion in a simplistic yet complicated way. I just want you to know that you have a choice and can choose what goes in and out of your wardrobe. Never force yourself to wear something you're uncomfortable in "just because..."

Remember that bright colors tend to enlarge and dark colors tend to diminish your figure. To feel more confident in determining what is right for you, discuss this topic with a "fashion-ready" friend. Think of someone you know who always looks fabulous in the right color or someone you trust to tell the truth about what looks good on you.

We all face apparel challenges at some point in our lives. However, if we cultivate variety in our wardrobe with the same enthusiasm that we do in our taste for different foods, we will be much further along in our image and personal style!

SECRET #4: Conduct a Closet Inventory

Do you have a closet full of clothes and nothing to wear? Over the years, this has become one of my "Got cha" questions that will get a room full of women talking at the same time. Although a custom-built closet would be a dream come true for many women, if it's stuffed with outdated clothes that no longer fit, getting dressed can be extremely frustrating—no matter how big or beautiful the closet.

What does your dream closet look like? Every shoe and sweater in place? Let me help you work toward your dream. You may or may not have a custom-designed closet in your budget, but something you must have is a plan. So let's do a closet inventory and clean the clutter. Once you do this, you'll know what garments you need and what you already have in order to build your new wardrobe.

In middle school, I had a Home Economics teacher tell me the way to prepare for gift giving is to always have wrapping paper and tissue on hand, as well as extra small gifts around so you're always prepared. I listened and still do this today.

I believe the same is true regarding our closets. We should have one or two outfits in our closet that will prepare us for any and all occasions. The cute and all-occasion black dress is a necessity for every woman. One that you can dress up for after-five, and the one you can wear to a surprise party. Make sure to carry this theme with purchases for all occasions. This means sporting events, weddings, professional events and the rest. Plan your purchases. Before going out on a shopping spree, carry a list of what you need.

Order in your surroundings and in your closet, not only helps you get to work on time but enables you to find that important piece for any special occasion without frustration. To organize your closet, first, clean the clutter by using cardboard boxes to categorize your clothing. Mark each of the boxes:

- Clean

- Repair/Alter

- Give Away

- Keep (These pieces will go back into your closet)

Next, remove all garments from your closet and sort through each item; checking for quality, cleanliness, repairs, fit and whether the color is right for you. Get rid of everything you haven't worn for more than two years. Your favorite charity will gladly accept it.

Put garments in the correct box and take them to the appropriate location so that you don't create more clutter for yourself. Don't forget to store seasonal clothing. Summer clothes should be properly stored for the winter and vice-versa if you live in an area where the seasons change.

Get rid of all wire hangers and purchase new ones in plastic, felt, wood, color, or design of your choice. Choose a color that will make you feel good about your new organizational system. Also purchase skirt, lingerie and belt hangers in coordinate colors.

Finally, hang and organize remaining items in the closet putting them in the following categories:

- Business blouses, shirts, and tops

- Business slacks and skirts

- Jeans, casual slacks and tops

- After-five and formal wear

- Hang or fold casual/sport shirts, shorts and swim wear

- Hang belts on belt hangers

- Organize handbags and shoes in easy-to-reach places

Create a place to store or hang scarves, and an organizer for jewelry. Purchase attractive stackable boxes for these.

Again, it's important to ditch wire hangers; even the ones from the cleaners. Re-hang dry cleaned clothes so that your closet doesn't look messy. Avoid wire hangers because they make unsightly imprints in garment shoulders and often do not hold their shape. Remember, an organized closet frees your mind to be more creative in choosing pieces when putting your daily look together.

SECRET #5: Know Your Body Type

Every woman has a unique body shape. Professionals use six body types to help women discover their unique category and determine what styles will balance imperfections and accentuate their best qualities.

Six Basic Body Shapes

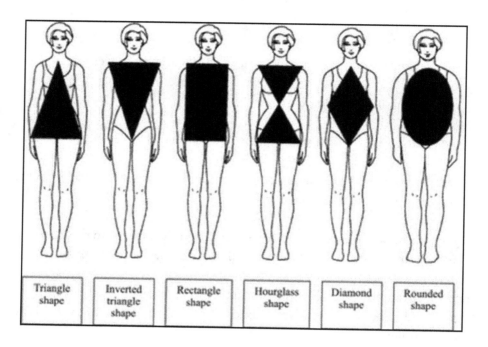

| Triangle shape | Inverted triangle shape | Rectangle shape | Hourglass shape | Diamond shape | Rounded shape |

The hourglass shape is considered the most desirable because the body appears balanced with proportionate measurements at the shoulders and hips. The bust will generally measure equal to the hips while the waist is 9-to-10-inches smaller. An example of a perfect hourglass figure is a 36-inch bust, 24-inch waist and 36-inch hips. The overall shape is curvy with a medium-to-large bustline. When choosing your fashion style, it's good to emphasize your waist. If you are petite, use vertical lines to elongate and create height.

The triangle (pear, spoon or bell-shape) has a narrow shoulder with a bust line that's two-to-four inches wider than the waist, and a hipline at least two-inches larger than the bust. This figure-type is wider at the hips and thighs than at the shoulder line with a flat tummy; often boasts of "no love handles" with a slender face and neck.

The inverted triangle shape (apple-shaped) is just the opposite of the triangle. This type has broad shoulders and bustline with a narrow waist and hips, often called a "swimmer's body." For this body-type, your figure is broadest through the bust, shoulders, and upper back. You should deemphasize your waist and bring balance to the hipline by wearing blouses that create a camouflage between the shoulder and hipline. Stay away from wearing a pencil skirt that would emphasize your broad shoulders. This is why wearing what's popular and fashionable for others may be wrong for you.

The rectangle figure-type shows little variance between the bustline, waist and hips, creating an overall columnar silhouette. This body-type may appear to have little or no waistline, measuring only six-to-eight inches smaller than the hip or bust. Athletic women who are runners often fit in this category. If this is your body-type, create the illusion of a waistline with a thin-belted or full-skirted look. This brings balance and adds dimension to the hips. You can also create a taller look by wearing black from shoulder-to-toe, which incorporates a strong vertical line. Styles with soft and gentle flared looks bring balance to the columnar silhouette.

The diamond has a wedge-type shape with a narrow shoulder and hipline. Most of your weight is distributed through the midriff and waist with a flat derriere. To balance your figure, shoulder pads and horizontal necklines add width to the shoulder. Make sure blouses taper-in from your bust and tummy to avoid the maternity look. Also avoid anything overly fitted, patterned and tailored through the waist.

The rounded figure is broader through the middle and upper torso with sloping shoulders and no waist indentation. The waist is full with a prominent tummy and sometimes flat derriere. You will want to deemphasize your waist and emphasize your shoulders, neck and face. Nice chunky jewelry works well and the tunic look with long verticals and asymmetrical lines are good. Don't try to create a waist where it doesn't exist, which only draws attention to your fullness. Instead, create the illusion of height by wearing V-necklines with straight and narrow skirts.

SECRET #6: Apply Line, Design & Color to Flatter Your Figure

Now that you know your body-type, you can flatter your figure by selecting complimentary lines and designs appropriate for your shape. These figure enhancers, which are called line, design, and color, help you create balance by accenting "assets" and minimizing "liabilities."

Creating balance where our shapes and figures appear "out of balance" has nothing to do with size or weight. Basically, an image consultant would do the following:

- Measure your body proportions: bust, waist, hips.

- Measure the length between the four quadrants of the body— Shoulder-to-waist; waist-to-hip (seven-inches down from the waist); hip-to-knee and knee-to-floor (barefooted).

- Ask what areas of your body cause you to be self-conscious.

- Determine solutions for camouflaging those areas.

- Inventory your wardrobe to identify what works and what needs to be purged.

- Make a shopping list, create a budget and timeline to purchase needed items.

Keep the following tips in mind...

- Vertical lines add length and height; horizontal lines add width, dimension and weight.

- Dark colors minimize and light colors enlarge—black and white are the bold examples.

- Floral designs add dimension but can diminish authority when worn by executive types.

- Bright colors can be used to accent and highlight. Do not use them on your "liabilities."

- Neutral colors can be used to marginalize and detract attention.

- The V-neck is the most slimming line for face and upper body.

- The round neckline will add weight and volume.

- Large designs and floral prints, bows and bright, bold colors undermine a professional look.

- Solid, dark and neutral colors are preferred for a business look.

Figure Challenges

We all need to create a balanced look. Some of us are short (below five-foot-two) with wide hips... Others have narrow hips with wide shoulders... And some are tall with seemingly no hipline or waist. The good news is... there's a fix for all shapes and body-types.

What to wear when you are ...

TALL (above 5'10")

If you want to appear shorter or reduce the appearance of your height, wear the following:

- Horizontal stripes—vertical strips cause you to appear taller

- Heavy, bulky fabrics if you are thin

- Hip length or three-quarter jackets

- Accessorize in relation to height—you can be very versatile

PETITE (5'2" and under)

If you want to appear taller, wear the following:

- Vertical lines and designs—from shoulder to your waist, hem or pant leg

- Create a vertical color line by wearing dresses in a solid color or by wearing matching color coordinates top-to-bottom

- Medium to small accessories, light weight jewelry

- Thin belts or no belt - simplicity in detail

- If you are petite, the length of your skirt is important. Skirts and dresses are most attractive at the knee or shorter.

THIN

You may want to appear more full-bodied—to accomplish this wear:

- Horizontal and curved lines are flattering for you—especially around the neckline when your face is thin.

- Full bodied, crisp and bulky fabrics can add inches wherever you need them.

- Layered and flowing looks can add drama and a vivacious look of high fashion.

- Puffy sleeves are cute and fun for summer looks.

- Accessorize in relation to height—tall and thin types look great in large, bulky and chunky jewelry with strappy and accentuated handbags.

- Wide belts can be flattering with ornamentation.

FULL-FIGURED/CURVY

Women who are full figured, many times feel challenged and insecure about how to dress their bodies with beauty and pizazz. You may want to appear thinner by following these tips:

- If you feel overweight or are unhappy about your hipline, styles and fabrics that skim, rather than hug the hipline are most flattering.

- Be careful with shiny fabrics that make the body appear larger.

- A V-neckline and pointed collars add length to the face. Creating a vertical line at the hip has a slimming effect.

- Introducing vertical lines in your top, bottom, skirt or dress will make the body appear taller and leaner.

- Vertical lines take away inches. Don't wear wide belts and ornamentation around the waist.

- When the face is full, hairstyles are important. Creating height with the hair is a cool way to soften and narrow the fullness of a round face.

I have a friend, Terri Murray, who is a full-figured model. She often states that for women with a full or round face, the plunging "V" neckline is perfect for bringing a slimming affect to the face and shoulder line. She also make the following statement on how line, design and color flatter full-figured women:

"I particularly like creating a vertical line with the same color bottom and top... and adding a signature jacket, shawl, kimono, or wrap. Creating a vertical color line gives a longer, slimming effect. You can also create the illusion of a smaller waist by adding a narrow belt under the jacket, shawl, kimono or wrap... If the lady has a full breast-line with wide shoulders and great legs, it would be a good choice for her to wear a skirt or dress above the knee."

SECRET #7: Understand Personality Styling

Personality is the totality of one's identity or behavior. Your "Personality Styling" is defined by your style in dress and how you express what's comfortable for you. We all have certain likes and dislikes about how we dress and usually fall into at least one of the following categories.

- DRAMATIC – As a trendsetter, you are a free spirit with a look characterized by fashion-forward designs and exotic eye-catching color combinations. You do not mind being the center of attention. Your expression in clothing is bold, bright, daring and different. You tend to wear ornate fashion jewelry and accessories with unusual designer shoes and handbags. You may also like unusual hairstyles, cuts and color highlights. Your makeup and nail polish are probably more daring than most.

- COUNTRY CASUAL – When shopping, flowery prints, ties and bows often catch your eye. You are attracted to clothing with lace and ruffles as well. You may even enjoy wearing full-long skirts. Some romantics really like the Victorian nostalgic look with vintage handbags and accessories. Buttoned-down shirts may seem stuffy and masculine to you. If you have a country flare, you may prefer fabrics like cotton, flannel and sometimes plaid. You prefer simple, understated makeup and nail polish.

- SPORTY – You prefer casual comfortable athletic clothes without any fuss or muss. You may prefer button-down collars, cotton blouses or athletic shirts rather than anything frilly or trendy. Perhaps a simple skirt, jeans, slacks or a tailored dress fits your style. Accessories may seem useless except for small post earrings and maybe a simple ring and bracelet. Because sporty types often love nature and being outdoors, you tend to prefer boots and flats heels. You do well with casual basic hairstyles paired with natural looking makeup.

- ALL-AMERICAN/CLASSIC –Your hair is usually cut with precision or pulled back for a controlled look. You enjoy traditional looks that never go out of style, and are extremely fussy about being well-groomed and neatly tailored. You insist on being coordinated and most often enjoy a conservative timeless style. You may prefer simple, elegant jewelry like pearls, gold or silver. You apply makeup carefully with skill and a light hand. You do it all with simplicity and elegance. No hoops, bangles and costume jewelry for you.

- TRENDSETTERS – You are usually motivated by current fashion trends and are in-step with what's new. You love free expression in dress and may choose what is most dazzling, trendy, unusual and exotic. You wear colorful bold costume jewelry with accessories and shoes that make a fashion statement. You may choose a toned down look for work, but will find a way to express your individual style without going overboard. Your style is very individualistic and won't be dictated by tradition.

- ECLECTIC – You usually borrow from different styles in dress to suit your mood. Most often, however, you are a "dramatic trendsetter" who can easily get bored with trendy looks. You are much happier using your creativity by switch up to match your mood. You may even borrow from two or three styles of dress to express something unique and different.

The six personality styles named here are simply guidelines that will provide a reference point to help you determine and define your personal preferences.

SECRET #8: Understand Investment Dressing

Invest wisely when shopping for items you want in your wardrobe. Look in your closet to see where you spend your fashion dollars. I once had a client who lived in the south, but loved jackets. Her closet was filled with jackets; some with sales tags still attached and others barely worn.

Let's be practical. Ask yourself these basic questions when spending your fashion dollar:

- Is the style right for my personality and figure?

- Is the garment and style appropriate for my lifestyle, profession and career?

- Is the color right for my skin tone, hair and eyes?

- Does it fit in all the right places, for all the right reasons?

- Will I get value and wear from this purchase?

Three Core Concepts for Investment Dressing

Evaluate your lifestyle and profession to determine where most of your time is spent, and where your investment dollars should go. If you are a news anchor, your wardrobe should convey a more business formal or business casual look depending on your network. On the other hand, if you are an architect, professional tennis player or an educator, your wardrobe will take on a business casual look. Evaluating your lifestyle is key to knowing where your wardrobe money should be spent. Styles convey different messages and are considered appropriate at certain places.

It's a good idea to keep a list of items you intend to purchase in your handbag. Be specific about the quality, colors, styles and the amount you want to pay, which keeps you from impulse buying. After all, many "storewide" door-buster sales are a ploy to sell cheaper merchandise that's been marked-up. Remember... invest wisely.

For a youthful look, don't be shy. You can create a fun-and-fabulous wardrobe with exciting coordinates that display the simplicity of the Three-F's of Fashion:

1. Flirty-fun and feminine to spice up your overall lady-like look.

2. Friendly-fabrics that do double-duty. They travel and wash well, and they cover and conceal flaws and imperfections.

3. Flattering—Flattering-figure-friendly fabrics that perfectly compliment women of any age, shape, weight, height or size.

Versatility is key to selecting the right style pieces for your wardrobe. Consider the fabric, whether it will keep its shape as well as what will be required for its care. As you know, these days, ironing is considered a chore we can do without.

If you have a limited budget, replace things little-by-little to make your signature look fun, flirty, and fabulous. Be mindful of the colors, fabrics, and fit that are best for you... your figure... and your personality style.

Finally, invest in quality rather than quantity. This includes accessories, such as jewelry, watches, belts, sassy hats (if you like wearing them), handbags and scarves, which can update the appearance of your wardrobe and add interest and color.

You may not shop at Tiffany's or Chanel, but you can still look regal on a tight budget. For a designer look, exceptional costume jewelry is abundantly available to accent, highlight and add pizazz to an otherwise ordinary look. All you need is creativity.

Fashion accent pieces give you a coordinated and finished look. It's best to purchase accessories when shopping for other items to better match colors, textures and styles. Begin the process...

- Start with determining where you spend your time (home, work, church, sports events). Make a chart. If you spend half of your time at work, half of your wardrobe should reflect this.

- Invest in quality jackets, blouses, scarves, sweaters or any item that focuses on the face as it gets more attention.

- Handbags, shoes and belts should be leather or a high quality "pleather" for casual.

- Before purchasing the garment, ask yourself: "Can I wear this for at least three years... in three different ways... on three different occasions?"

- If you're just beginning to seriously invest in a quality wardrobe, begin with neutral and solid colors starting with black, gray, navy, brown and beige for the basics. Then add some fun and zesty color accents using belts, handbags and jewelry with a sassy pair of flats or boots.

- If you are on a budget, choose classic and basic styles over trendy looks. Trends are short-lived. Go for the look that lasts.

Be sure to make this a fun and exciting experience. Investing time and energy into a transformative new you is not only rewarding personally; but, can be uplifting to those who matter the most in your life.

CHAPTER SEVEN

DINING WITH DIGNITY

At a dinner party we should eat wisely, but not too well,
and talk well, but not too wisely.
–Somerset Maugham

CELEBRATIONS, PARTIES, AND sharing a meal with friends are part of life's simple pleasures. I love having people over to enjoy a special meal—adding special touches like music, decorative plates, candlelight, and flowers. This always sparks my creativity and brightens my day. But, most importantly, I get to show appreciation, catch up on their activities—and it provides an opportunity to share some love.

The word of God places all humanity in a category called families. The word "family" denotes relationship. From the beginning, it was his intent that we learn to be relational. In the household of the family, there is kinship—either by blood or by familial relationship. Because we are all so very different in culture and society, this take intentional work.

The Bible says in Luke 7:17 that a house divided against itself shall not stand. One of the ways we build relationship in a household is by eating together. Jesus showed us this when he was on earth as he built strong relationships with his disciples. There are times when families solve disputes and make important decisions around a cup of coffee and a slice of cake. Making time to exchange ideas—sharing different points of view is central to building cohesive relationships.

When the first century church began, Acts 2:46 says that the believers went from house to house breaking bread together. Just imagine if local churches and communities reestablished this tradition. Communities would be literally transformed so that the kingdom of God could truly thrive on earth—in every township and community. Children would learn scripture from parents and relatives—not just from the pulpit at church or a Bible app. Just imagine if we were to enact God's plan.

In this chapter, you'll find detailed guidelines and tips to brush-up on your social entertaining and dining etiquette skills. Whether you're setting a table for a special occasion or mastering the art of social discourse while dining, you will not only become proficient with hosting a meal, but feel more comfortable attending formal events.

Colorful napkins and placemats add interest to your table. No time to set the table? Have it pre-set and reward yourself by using actual tableware versus plastic and paper plates. This makes mealtime more meaningful. Paper plates and plastic ware are fine in a pinch or for a picnic. However, when your aunt comes to visit from out of town, take the time to honor her by giving her the royal treatment.

Because life is so busy and time with loved ones is often limited, mealtime is an ideal occasion for pleasant conversation—to catch-up and check-in with one another without the distraction of cellphones and social media. Family and friends need to know they are special.

Although social distancing has curtailed eating meals together, hopefully, this season of our lives will be short-lived. Setting the table, adding fresh flowers and even setting the atmosphere with music will help your family and guests relax and enjoy spending time together. Children also recognize these cues as they grow-up and learn the importance of giving attention to make social gatherings a special time.

INFORMAL DINING

Informal dining may only consist of soup and sandwiches, yet care and pre-planning are essential to make everyone feel special and enjoy the experience. When entertaining, be sensitive to what others like and enjoy. A savvy host asks what type of music his or her guests like... pop, country, jazz, gospel or classical music? A gracious hostess accommodates her guests.

It's rude to insist that your guests listen to your favorite music, or entertainment or that they eat your favorite food. If they love Bach and are vegetarian, make the effort to listen to and serve their favorites for the evening. Listen to your country music and enjoy a juicy steak another time. You can always ask your guest or guests before you plan your menu what they enjoy eating so that you can make it an evening they will long remember—for all the right reasons.

How to Set the Table

The illustration above shows a simple place setting for lunch or dinner with both a salad and dinner plate. Because of the dinnerware and implements shown, we can determine that a salad or soup is on the menu, as well as a main dish and dessert. Most likely, after the salad is eaten, a bowl of soup will be served if the guest chooses to partake.

When setting the table for guests, note the following:

- A nicely set table has food, sauces, or beverages in dishes and pitchers. Never place cartons of milk and juice, salt-and-pepper boxes, jelly jars or butter in the wrapper on the table.

- Use placemats and coasters if a table cloth is not in use. Placemats and coasters will keep your table free from crumbs and moisture. Do not use placemats on a tablecloth.

- Place the napkin either to the left of the plate or on the plate. Use a napkin holder for color and accent.

- The plate should be one inch from the edge of the table. If you look closely, the salad plate is placed on the dinner plate in the illustration above. It is also acceptable to place it to the right of the plate.

- The charger is partly decorative and is useful as well to keep the table free from crumbs and sauces.

- Knives and spoons are set to the right of the plate. The butter knife is placed on the bread plate.

- Forks are placed to the left side of the plate with the tines-up.

- Informal dining may or may not include a salad knife. Many times, the salad fork is reserved for formal dining.

- Both a dinner fork and knife should be available for a meal. Most foods are eaten with a fork, but a knife is handy for cutting and for pushing food onto one's fork.

- Place your bread and butter plate above the fork or forks, on the left side of the plate. Place the butter knife on the bread plate if one is available.

- Beverages are always to the right of the plate. Place the water goblet or glass at the tip of the knife, and the tea or coffee cup is to the right of the water glass. Often a coffee cup is not placed on the table until dessert is served.

- Do not fill glasses to the top. Fill them only three-fourths full so it's easier to drink.

- Silverware is used from the outside-inward. The placement of forks and knives indicate menu items served first. For example, when the salad fork is placed outside the dinner fork, the salad will be served before the entree.

- A soup spoon to the right of the teaspoon indicates that soup or stew will be served for an appetizer or main course.

- If salad or soup is not served, there's no need to put a salad fork or soup spoon on the table.

- Always wait until everyone is seated, and grace is offered before eating. The hostess will pick up her napkin to signal when the meal is to begin.

HOW TO EAT FINGER FOODS

With fast food restaurants everywhere and the busyness of life, it's much more convenient to grab a sandwich and go. When dining in a hurry or informally, remember the following:

- Hors d'oeuvres—Place sauces and dips on your plate rather than dipping from the serving dish.

- Bacon, French fries and crispy fried chicken—if crisp, use your fingers. If not, use a fork and knife.

- Corn on the cob—Served with casual meals. Butter the corn and season several rows at a time. Use both hands to hold the cob, being careful not to spray others while eating.

- Eggs—Hard-cooked eggs are eaten with a fork. Soft-cooked eggs are eaten directly from the shell with a spoon. Slice the top with a knife.

- Bananas—Peel and eat with a knife-and-fork at the table.

- Berries—Eaten with a spoon. Large strawberries served with the stem are held by the stem, dipped in sugar and eaten in two bites.

- Grapefruit—Halves are served with sections loosened and eaten with a spoon. Do not attempt to squeeze out the juice except in the privacy of your own home.

- Oranges—Peeled with a sharp knife and eaten in sections. If peeled and served on a plate, the orange is eaten with a fork.

- Fruit & cheese—Cut fresh fruit and soft-cheese with a knife-and-fork.

PSST...YOUR MANNERS ARE SHOWING

Table manners matter. Whether in public or at home, the person most respected and admired is the one who is courteous and mannerly in everyday dealings, and at the dinner table.

Spend time with young children and teens setting the table and practicing good table manners. They will always make a good impression when dining out if they know what is appropriate and how to conduct themselves in the company of others.

The dinner table reveals a lot about a person—whether they are selfish, patient, careful, good listeners and considerate. Are they refined individuals who have been taught good manners; or are they disciplined enough to even care?

Someone who slurps his or her tea or coffee, after reaching over other guests for a larger slice of pie is automatically marked as a "never again" dinner guest.

Then, there's the person who licks their fingers after pushing their meat on the fork... and the person who uses their knife-and-fork as a baton during conversation—waving it around like a flag to make a point.

It is hard to invite annoying dinner guests to a special meal without remembering the last time. On the other hand, we tend to savor pleasant memories with guests who are polite and aware of dining etiquette.

- In a private residence, the hostess should suggest where to leave a handbag and or coat.

- If a guest prefers to bring her handbag to the table, she should hang it on the chair, place it on the floor, or on her lap. Never place personal items on the table.

- Never come to the table or a social event chewing gum. Use mints instead.

- The host or hostess are seated at opposite ends of the table.

- Ladies with an escort should be seated to the left of the gentleman. Ladies should sit and rise from the chair's left-side.

- Alternate men and women around the table when possible. A male guest of honor sits to the right of the hostess. A female guest of honor sits to the right of the host.

- Unless couples or individuals insist on sitting together, it's perfectly acceptable for married couples and other partners to sit apart.

- Be patient and wait for the invocation or prayer. If none is given, silently pray over your meal.

- Never call attention to yourself by wiping your utensils with your napkin or cleaning them with water before dining. If you find that a utensil isn't clean, simply ask for a replacement.

- It's important to hold a fork or spoon correctly. Hold your fork or your spoon between your thumb and forefinger... like a pencil.

- Cutting food in small pieces before eating, or mixing food together on your plate does not show good manners. Cut one bite at a time.

- Do not rest elbows on the table, stretch your feet out under the table or talk with food in your mouth. Rest your hand and arm in your lap.

- Don't use condiments before tasting your food—especially at someone's home. (The chef takes pride in cooking so taste first)

- Toothpicks or floss are never used at the table or in public. Cleaning your teeth should be done in private. If food gets lodged in your teeth, drink a sip of water to be discreet, or excuse yourself and go to the restroom.

- Some salads have large chunks of lettuce, carrots, and other veggies. Cut large chunks into bite size pieces before putting them in your mouth. Cherry tomatoes, if bite size can be eaten whole.

- Although you may not like a dish, you should at least try it, and not comment on what you do or do not like.

- Always keep dinner conversation pleasant. This is not the time to discuss life's difficulties and controversial matters.

- Never pick up a bowl or saucer to eat or drink from it. Leave all dinnerware in place while dining.

- Never place used utensils on the table. Place them on your plate between bites, while chewing, or breaking bread.

- Use the bread plate or your dinner plate to butter your bread. Never put bread or any food, on the tablecloth or your napkin while dining.

- Bread or rolls should be broken into halves and or quarters, depending on the size, and buttered with the bread or dinner knife. Toast should be cut in-half and buttered one piece-at-a-time.

- Place butter, or jam on your bread plate before spreading it on your bread. Never butter your bread directly from the butter dish. Once you place butter or jam on your plate, remember to pass it to others. If you don't have a bread plate, place your bread, butter or jam directly on your plate.

- When passing food, hold the dish while the person next to you serves him or herself. It's polite to allow others to go first.

- As mentioned earlier, use your knife as a "pusher" to place or push food on your fork.

- Cut your food in bite-size pieces as you eat small bites. It's rude to shovel-down food without looking up to enjoy conversation.

- After stirring coffee or tea, place the spoon on your saucer. Do not slurp beverages... it is extremely annoying to others.

- Place utensils in a resting position while chewing and conversing, by putting them on the upper right edge of your plate in a diagonal position, with the blade of the knife facing-in, toward your plate.

- If your knife or any other utensil is not needed during the meal, it's perfectly fine to leave it on the table until you have finished your meal.

- You may cut soft food like pancakes or meatloaf with a fork.

- When dining family style, ask for food and other items to be passed to you. Do not reach over someone's plate.

- Cut around fat, gristle or bone and push it to the side...or remove with your fingers, not your napkin.

- When cutting meat, hold the knife in the right-hand, and the fork in the left with the tines down... Or the opposite if left-handed. Cut your meat with a slicing motion, picking-up the knife and placing it properly to cut one slice at a time. Cutting the meat in small pieces all at once is fine, if you're helping a small child, but not at an adult party.

- After cutting your meat, switch hands to take a bite, passing the fork to the right-hand, if you're right-handed or vice-versa for left-handed persons.

- Again, always use a knife for cutting. Never place your fingers on foods unless they are finger-foods.

- Eat most dinner foods with a fork (vegetables, rice, potatoes). Eat most fruits, custards and puddings with a spoon (peach, strawberry slices, yogurt). Very crispy bacon, fries and whole strawberries are considered finger-foods.

- Do not ask for or share food from someone's plate unless it's your spouse or a child in an informal setting.

- If you drop your napkin, or utensil on the floor, ask for another. When finished, loosely fold your napkin next to your plate.

- Never arrange your hair or apply lipstick, gloss or makeup at the table.

- Finally, when finished with your meal, place your utensils in a "4:20" position on your plate, with the knife-blade facing center.

FORMAL DINING

Investing the time and even money to learn the intricacies of formal dining will pay untold dividends in building your level of confidence on special occasions and when dining out. Knowing what to expect... what to say... what to do... without fear or intimidation prepares you to successfully dine in ritzy restaurants and at fancy banquets.

Not following formal dining etiquette doesn't mean you commit the cardinal sin... but brushing-up on your dining skills is important if you aspire to do impressive things with important people.

As a host or hostess for a formal meal, planning and thinking through all the details is key to hosting a fabulous occasion. I like to put myself in my guests' shoes by mentally rehearsing the event—planning out each detail.

When dining in a special setting, the first thing to do is to introduce yourself, get acquainted, and then sit down to enjoy the meal. Make sure you take note of special seating if there are seating designations.

Once you sit down, what next? Let's review the implements in front of you, which might include a charger or service plate. Here you will find an illustration of how a formal dinner table might be set and where to find the different place ware on the table.

As I mentioned before, you may find a "charger" where the plate is normally placed. A charger is a decorative plate. It is there for keeping crumbs, drips and sauces from soiling the table. It is also called the "cover plate," or "service plate." Your salad and dinner plate will be placed on this plate. It will be removed before serving dessert.

The other implements, or eating utensils in a formal place setting will ordinarily include a dessert spoon and fork, multiple glasses and a variety of knives and forks.

- The dessert implements... spoon and or fork are above the plate. If cake or pie is served, you will find a fork in the dessert position. If custard or cobbler is served, a spoon would be appropriate. If cake and ice cream are served, you will find both a spoon and fork.

- The water goblet and or beverage glass should be at the tip of the knife. Red, white wine and champagne glasses can be found above the spoons. The coffee cup is sometimes not placed on a formal table. It is brought in last with dessert. If placed on the table, you will find it to the right of the spoon.

- When sitting at a crowded table, it's easy to pick up the wrong cup or glass. Just remember that your water can be found at the tip of your knife... on the right side of your plate... and your coffee cup, if on the table, can be found to the right of your spoon.

- Several more things are very important when dining in a formal setting. Wait until the host and or hostess is seated before you sit. Also be aware of reserved seating. Another important point; do not pick up your napkin or knife and or fork until the host or hostess picks up his or hers. They are the ones from whom you are taking ques. The napkin is always placed on your lap before beginning to eat your meal.

- Gently place your forefingers over the glass or cup to indicate that you don't want a refill or simply say, "No, thank you."

- Always pass to the right of your position. Pass the salt and pepper together. Pass pitchers or gravy boats by turning the handle toward the person receiving it.

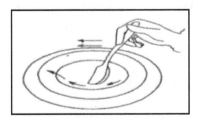

- Always spoon soup away from you to help avoid spills.

- When having coffee or tea and conversation after dinner, keep your napkin in your lap. Placing a soiled napkin on the table while others are still holding a conversation may seem to indicate that you are impatient.

- To prevent heavy lipstick stains on glasses and cups, blot your lipstick before coming to the table.

- If you don't like the food served, be polite and do not make rude comments or show dislike... simply try it.

- If you can't suppress a burp or sneeze, cover your nose and mouth with your napkin and say, "Excuse me."

- If a bug crawls out of your salad or a fly lands in your tea, don't sicken others and embarrass your host... ask for another salad or cup of tea.

- When finished with your meal, don't push your plate away and don't stack your dishes. Leave your plates and bowls in position and place your implements in the "4:20" position mentioned earlier.

FIRST CLASS FORMAL

If you are attending a Statehouse dinner, a formal meal at the Governor's mansion or some other elite and prestigious event, you will need to know what an individual salt and pepper shaker might look like and where you might find the menu card. I suggest that you always be prepared for the unexpected. The "first class formal" setting includes even more implements, glasses and other appointments.

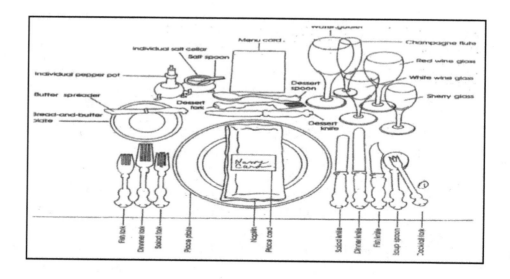

In 1996, on a business trip to Washington, D.C., I had the opportunity to make an appointment with a girlfriend, who at the time, worked in the White House as an administrative aide to President Bill and Hillary Clinton.

She invited me to have lunch in the President's dining room. Indeed, it had never occurred to me that I would have this privilege. The Clinton's happened to be out of town; however, because of former training, I believe I would have been prepared. We never know when a once in a life-time opportunity might arise. For this reason, we must consistently invest in our personal and spiritual growth so that we can live up to our heavenly calling as ambassadors for the Lord Jesus Christ.

While visiting, my friend gave me a tour of the oval office. I had an opportunity to casually chat with the former President's secretary, Betty Curry. She was cordial and gracious. I tried to capture every moment, learning as much as possible about the various rooms and their significance. I took photos; but, I cannot emphasize enough the importance of preparation.

A friend once shared that—success is the point where preparation and opportunity meet. Here you will find more tips for social and dining success:

- Gentlemen escort ladies with her right arm linked through his left.

- The host or hostess is the first person to be seated and then other guests. Never switch name cards to be seated next to a preferred guest without permission.

- Once seated, be cautious, holding your elbows close to your body so no one gets poked while dining.

- If you are being introduced while seated at the table, simply smile and nod to acknowledge the introduction. You are not required to stand—this is especially true of ladies.

- During times of social distancing, rather than standing to shake hands—if a gentleman or lady is being introduced to someone passing by your table, it may be less disruptive to simply smile, nod and raise your hand to acknowledge a dignitary. If protocol requires that you stand, do so.

- Once seated, half-fold the dinner napkin on you lap. Place open corners facing your body to easily open… and stay free of crumbs, sauces and other mealtime annoyances. This is a clever way to hide the soiled portion between the folds.

- Once all guests are seated and it's time for the meal to begin, you can expect the hostess or host to unfold her napkin halfway and place it on her lap to indicate the start of the meal.

- Refrain from helping yourself to bread or beginning to eat your salad before your host begins. The hostess should begin eating when all guests are served. It's considerate to ask if everyone has been served before taking a bite.

- Napkins are never tucked into a shirt or blouse. Likewise, it's inappropriate to throw a tie over the shoulder or tuck it into a shirt to avoid spills. Careful dining shouldn't require the extras that draw attention to mealtime indiscretions.

- Formal meals are generally served in three-to-four courses. The first is usually soup and bread.

- Never snap your fingers, clap, wave your napkin or tap the glass to get the attention of the service person. This is considered extremely rude and disrespectful. Instead, lift your finger and say, "Excuse me, may I have…"

- When someone asks a question while your mouth is full, just smile nicely while chewing… point to your mouth so the question can be redirected to someone else or asked later.

- At the end of a meal, if you are at a restaurant, sign the check away from your guest and place it face down. Determine who will pay for the meal before guests arrive and notify the server.

- When you are finished, loosely fold your napkin and place it next to your plate.

BEVERAGE TIPS

- Hold chilled white wines by the glassware stem to keep fingertips from warming the glass.

- Hold red table wines such as Rose', Burgundy, Bordeaux, Chianti and Zinfandel by the glass as they aren't chilled.

- Red wines are ordered to compliment red meat, i.e., beef, pork and lamb. White wines are ordered to compliment fish, poultry and seafood.

DEALING WITH DIFFICULT FOODS

Lobster—The claws are cracked with a nutcracker. The meat is extracted with a seafood fork, dipped in butter or sauce and eaten. Ask to have it cracked in the kitchen.

Stuffed Lobster—Eaten with a knife and fork.

Shrimp—A finger-food eaten by holding the tail to dip in sauces bitten off... the tail is discarded.

Shrimp Cocktail (Jumbo)—Eaten with a seafood fork. Eat large shrimp in two bites, or on serving plate and cut with a fork to dip into the sauce.

Hard Shelled Crab—Eaten with a knife and fork.

Soft Shell Crab—Eat the entire item.

Clams (fried)—Eaten with a fork.

Fresh Oysters, Mussels and Clams—Use a fish or oyster fork for oysters, mussels and clams served on the half-shell. Hold the shell with one hand and remove the oyster, mussel or clam whole with the fork.

Snails—If tongs are provided, hold shell with tongs and pull out snail with oyster fork. Otherwise, hold shell with fingers. The snail is eaten whole. You may dip your bead in garlic butter.

AMERICAN VS CONTINENTAL DINING

There are two main dining styles in Western countries: "American" and "Continental." The "American" style is what we've discussed so far... the fork is placed in either your right or left-hand when you eat. When cutting meat or other foods, the knife is held in either the right or left-hand. After cutting, the knife is put in the 4:20 position... then food is eaten with the fork in your right or left-hand.

When dining "Continental" style, eat with the fork in your left hand, using the knife as a pusher to place food on the back of the fork. The main difference between the two dining styles is the positioning of the knife and fork. Dining "American" style requires switching back-and-forth, while dining "Continental" style requires that utensils stay in the same hand. This style seems more practical to some diners.

UNDERSTANDING RESTAURANT TERMINOLOGY

We know that the polite and courteous person at the dinner table earns the most respect; but, the person who is knowledgeable about dining terminology in a classy restaurant isn't far behind. So, first understand that if you do not see a price on the menu, be prepared to pay top-dollar for your meal. Don't ask how much—just enjoy the meal and prepare to dig-deep. Ordinarily items that are not priced are ordered a la carte—meaning they are priced and ordered individually and not priced as part of a meal.

- Main Course: A choice between up to four dishes.

- Entree: The main course in the U.S. includes meat, fish or fowl.

- Full Course Meal: A dinner consisting of three or four courses or more, i.e., hors d'oeuvres, soup, and dessert.

- Fixed Price: Set price for the entrée, which may or may not include side dishes.

- Market Price: Ask waiter for current price (e.g. the price of fish may vary depending upon the time of year).

MENU TERMINOLOGY

A la—a French term meaning "in the style of."

A la carte—each dish is priced and ordered individually.

A la king—chopped food, usually chicken or turkey in cream sauce with sliced mushrooms and pimiento.

A la mode—pie or dessert topped with a scoop of ice cream. Almandine—made or served with almonds or nuts.

Appetizer—food served before the main meal... usually shared.

Au gratin—a dish that's browned in an oven or broiler topped with buttered breadcrumbs, grated cheese or both.

Au jus—food, usually roast beef served in its own juices.

Bisque—a thick creamy soup.

Bouillabaisse (boo-ee-ya-bays)—a fish and shellfish soup.

Butterfly—to split food down the center but not all the way through so that the two halves can be opened flat like butterfly wings.

Café au lait—coffee with milk or cream.

Canapé—small pieces of toast covered with food spread.

Carte du jour—menu of the day.

Cordon Blue—filled with cheese, ham or Canadian bacon.

Crepe—thin French pancakes.

Du jour—means "of the day," like soup du jour.

En brochette—food that is cooked on a skewer.

Flambé—desserts soaked in liquor and set ablaze.

Fricassee—describes chicken or small game that is cooked in sauce with vegetables after first being cut up and browned.

Garnish—Eatable flowers or other decorative items or toppings to add appeal to a dish, food or the meal.

Gazpacho—a cold soup that is tomato-based with uncooked vegetable garnish.

Hors d' oeuvres—foods served as appetizers.

Julienne—cut in thin strips.

Manhattan clam chowder—tomato-based chowder.

New England clam chowder—white and creamy clam soup.

Puree—to grind to paste either by pressing through a food mill or whirling in a food-processor.

Marinate—to steep meat, fish, fowl, vegetables or other food in a spicy liquid for several hours until the food absorbs the flavor.

Ragout (ra-goo)—a hearty stew of seasoned meat and vegetables.

Saute'—to fry in a small amount of fat or hot oil.

Soufflé—very light egg mixture, whipped to a froth, baked until puffy.

Vichyssoise (vee-shee-swawz)—the 'se' has a 'z' sound)—a cold pureed potato and leeks soup.

CELL PHONE ETIQUETTE

Keep conversation light and pleasant at mealtime, and cell phones on vibrate or turned off unless you're expecting an urgent call. Parents must remember that your children, teens and family members are watching you. If you insist on texting during meals, they are likely to do the same.

Let brotherly love continue. Be not forgetful to entertain
(means to receive in an hospitable way) strangers: for thereby
some have entertained angels unawares.
—Hebrews 13:2

Remember that mealtime should be a special time to focus on those with whom you are dining. Scripture teaches us that opportunities to connect with a brother or sister can be considered a divine moment. Angels are divine messengers. Think again about the many times you dined or had coffee with a believer. You may have been more engaging or committed to conversation if you had been more spiritually in tune. You would have known it was meant to be a divine set up!

If you are expecting an important call, simply excuse yourself when the call comes in; stepping away to a private area. Try to keep the conversation brief so that your absence does not disrupt the flow of the meal. Much can be missed in five minutes of conversation.

Always put technical devices in your pocket or purse rather than on the table. It's rude to text or review social media while dining; unless you are conducting urgent business. The bottom line is this—when we know what to do and how to conduct ourselves at mealtime, our friends and acquaintances will welcome our company.

Being acquainted with how to dine comfortably, no matter the situation or setting is key to being known as an exceptionable host and guest. Anyone can be mediocre, however, kingdom women seek to do and be more. They excel in all they do because they invest time and effort into loving others as Christ loved us—unconditionally.

Because we are representatives of the kingdom, we go beyond simply being acceptable—we are exceptional. Living on an ambassadorial plane requires more of us than a quick meal at McDonalds and Chick-fila-A. Confident and classy kingdom women are at ease whether interviewing in a classy restaurant or when out on a date. Because they've become acquainted with what is required to make every social encounter a pleasant one, we are reasonably prepared. After all, as a VIP in the kingdom, we are God's masterpiece. We are royalty. So, Lady Love, put on your imaginary crown. You've got this!

CHAPTER EIGHT

THE GET NOTICED WOMAN

JUST LOVE WALKING into a unique store like the Merz Apothecary in downtown Chicago, which boasts of having one of the largest collections of natural and luxury soaps from around the world under one roof. The shop window looks rather ordinary. What can be found on the inside, however, is extraordinary.

If you want to make a woman smile, give her a beautiful fragrance made with lemon oil, rose oil, or a touch of lavender. Mertz offers luscious fragrances from around the world—enough to make any woman believe that living lavishly is her portion.

A first-class woman of God is one of God's most precious gifts to the earth. She has set her sights on excellence. Because she is committed to the high calling that is in Christ Jesus, she is committed to discipline and foresight. She achieves more, because she requires more—not only of herself, but, of others. Disciplining myself to learn the "insider secrets" I've shared in the last chapter, my hunger to pursue a life in the spirit has required a life-time quest that I might be my best for God. I live my life as a sacrificial offering—to share as much as I can with others—so they too can be their best for God. After all, He's worth it—and so are you.

I've written seven chapters already. They contain valuable nuggets known to professional image-makers around the world and are the foundational tools designed to help women design a signature look and presence to impress. The unique and distinct qualities of "the get noticed woman" of God will cause her to stand out wherever she goes. Within her loins lies destiny, legacy and the foundations of culture and society. She is rich with potential.

The fragrance we bring to the world is unique. Our male counterparts have their unique contribution, and we have ours. We all arrive in varied shades, hues and with varied body structures. As women, we dazzle and amaze because we are his masterpiece. We did not choose him—he chose us for his purpose; to nurture human life and potential. As we grow and mature, influencing those we touch, we fulfill God's dream. We are His conduit—filling the earth with His love and affection.

Mature women; not necessarily in age, but in our ability to be transformed by His word, have a specific assignment in the earth. This mandate and call is spelled out in Titus 2:3. It is important to note that the essential role of mature men of God as a teacher and mentor is most appropriately outlined first. After listing character qualities of men of God, the qualities and requirements of mature women are listed. I have taken the time to provide a paraphrased rendering.

Titus 2:3 is a passage written by Paul to Titus, his mentee in the gospel. The passage is addressing mature women of God. We are being strongly urged to be holy, pure and honorable—not being slanderous; but, temperate in the use of wine and to be teachers of good things.

As women of maturity in the body of Christ, we are also given this exhortation: *They must teach younger women to love their husbands and children, be discreet, know how to manage their homes and be respectful to their husbands so that the word of God and people of God are not given a bad name.*

The Apostle Paul is not just teaching here, but, making an appeal, by way of Titus. He is making a plea; placing a demand on those of us who know God's word, to behave with faith in action; as those who set an example. We are being encouraged to live a life-style that honors God in an excellent and influential way to reflect his name and nature.

We are being reminded here that we are to show ourselves as a "pattern of good works." In modern-day terms, this means presenting ourselves as role models; both in speech and behavior.

Make no mistake about it, we are precious and rare gifts to the world… irreplaceable and one of a kind. As light-bearers we are a life-giving source to those who stumble in darkness. In our own homes, we are raising children and grandchildren who need our guidance. There are limitless opportunities for the get noticed woman to make a difference in the lives of others.

Although a woman's outward beauty can be apparent at first glance, the core of the woman—her heart of gold and love for God are the real treasures to behold. God speaks of us as his temple—or dwelling place. What a privilege to bear His name and presence.

The Bible often speaks of the Holy Spirit inside as hidden treasure. II Corinthians 4:6 & 7 from the Amplified version, speaks of this hidden treasure as a light that has the potential to shine forth in majesty and glory.

For God who said, Let light shine out of darkness, has shone in our hearts so as to bring forth light for the illumination of the knowledge of the majesty and glory of God (as it is manifested and revealed) in the face of Jesus Christ the Messiah.

Vs 7: However, we possess this precious treasure (the divine light of the gospel) in (frail, human) vessels of earth that the grandeur and exceeding greatness of the power may be shown to be of God and not from ourselves.

The Merz boutique has a tradition of shipping gift packages that are unique in design, color and fragrance to their customers all over the world. So it is with the woman who taps into her own personal and unique gift-package—the inner core of who she is. These treasures leave behind a fragrant reminder of her presence wherever she goes. Those around her know they can be uplifted and encouraged by her giftedness, simply because the atmosphere always changes when she is near.

When I think of the word "fragrance," I think of a scripture that has always fascinated me:

II Corinthians 2:14 & 15: (NIV paraphrased): But thanks be to God, who always leads us triumphantly in Christ and through us spreads everywhere the fragrance of the knowledge of him. For we are to God the aroma of Christ among those who are being saved and those who are perishing.

What a beautiful mind picture. God speaks to us through His word to let us know that when we are saved—accept Jesus as Lord—that the fragrance of the knowledge of him is being aromatically spread everywhere like a fragrant perfume. Did you know that when you embrace the knowledge of

God in Christ, that you are not only to others; but also to God like a sweet smelling aroma? How beautiful.

Our lives have not only a body and soul dimension—but a spiritual essence that energizes everything we touch. The spiritual dimension is the core of *you*. Without this key element of a woman's life, what could be vital and enriched is dead and without life.

Although the previous chapters focus on our appearance and behavior, please understand that the engine behind the true get noticed woman is her life in the spirit. I want my readers to know that without the spiritual dimension coming to life, we have no chance of becoming complete and whole.

My life has been blessed, beautified, and "fragranced" by countless women and men who have mentored, counselled, and advised me. They offered their support and encouragement, helping me to make strides to advance the kingdom. In turn, I've had countless opportunities to bring hope and healing to women and girls, opening pathways to bright visions of a fragrant joy-filled future. This reciprocal journey is what God had in mind from the beginning. We cannot be our best all alone.

The women and men who have made the most significant contributions in my life have all been born-again Christians. They have been confidants and prayer warriors who fully understood the core of who I am and recognized the importance of my desire to make faith fully known in the marketplace. The way we treat one another and stand tall on our values are key attributes of the get noticed woman. When we make known our sincere desire to grow in God, our heavenly Father provides faith-partners and support.

Just like the fragrances sent far and wide from the Merz to deliver a sweet aroma from city to countryside, so it is the fragrance of my service through coaching, mentoring and ministry has impacted the lives of many. The gifts I share have been cultivated and nurtured to bless the lives of those within my realm of influence. In a personalized way, the gifts we offer to the world as women are unique and precious. When we know Christ, no matter where we go, we leave an aromatic and sweet-smelling fragrance that radiates from a heart of love.

THE BEAUTY IN THE BUD

In the early 1990s, I spent several years working as a pageant judge and wardrobe consultant in Fayetteville, North Carolina. Young ladies would come to me for coaching—often with extremely low self-esteem. Quite frankly, my job could have been summed up as a "confidence builder."

Weeks later, they would leave my studio with a new attitude regarding their potential. Their countenance had noticeably changed. They had a new-found confidence that was unquestionably beautiful. Working with them became less about "making girls beautiful" and more about setting the stage for beautiful possibilities to emerge.

Young girls need parents and mentors to help them look and feel their best. The home is where foundations are built to help them reach their full potential. If they don't get the affirmations and support they need early on, these budding beauties began to suffer from low self-esteem.

In raising my own daughters, as well as working with hundreds of youth in various school classrooms and in my non-profit, The Gold Medallion Foundation, I made a discovery. For more than 20 years, I taught, advised and coached. What I have been blessed to discover is that all children and adults have a need for attention.

Some of us simply need a smile or a big hug. Many of us also need encouragement, affirming words, guidance and direction. Although we hide and try to reassure others that we are just fine; deep down inside we are all reaching out for affirming words, attention—something more. Often enough, we don't want to admit how deeply we are hurting; and how empty we really feel inside. The trauma, pressures and delays in life often shatter our dreams. Proverbs 13:12 offers encouragement for each of us:

> *Hope deferred (delayed) makes the heart sick (causes discouragement), but, when the desire cometh, it is a tree of life.*

This scripture describes a sickness we have all felt—sickness of mind, heart and emotion. Some of us desire to be married, want a soul mate, a child; want to be healed of a terminal disease and more. Some of us have experienced disappointment and heartbreak so many times, we want to give up. We've waited and waited, yet the answer never seems to come. Some are still waiting, but, we all must remember that God is faithful and will answer in due season. He is never early, nor late; but is always right on time.

My first book, *"Get Noticed! Insider Secrets to a Confident and Classy Image"* was written as an alert. I wanted women to know that it's time to shake off the fears and apprehensions we've harbored and nurtured over time. It's time to be released from our prisons and claim our giftedness. One of my favorite musicians wrote this statement on her CD cover, "Shine."

> *"...and the day came when the risk it took to remain tight in a bud was more painful than the risk it took to blossom."*
> –Shana Tucker

Isn't it time kingdom women began to open up? Isn't it time to release the pain? This book, *"The Get Noticed Woman: Keys to Kingdom Influence & Excellence,"* is designed to define the woman of God who can significantly impact the world by owning her power and potential. Her gifts and talents as a kingdom educator and mentor are needed perhaps more than ever.

I love roses. I've noticed over the years that when I grow roses, they take considerable intentional care. God knew that the same is true about us as human beings. That's why He not only said He would never leave nor forsake us, but He gave us not only a natural family, but, in addition, members of the body of Christ for guidance and support. He thought of everything. It is my heart to encourage my sisters in Christ to embrace all that He has given us.

Although it takes time and patience to bring forth the beauty and fragrance of a rose—or any flower—it's worth it. The giftedness and beauty of a woman does not happen overnight. But if we have no idea what we are striving for, there is no motivation to do the work.

For many of us, there seems to be too few role models. Women who truly love God appreciate having good examples to follow. Not everyone has a good mother or grandmother in their life. Without a guiding hand, it's all too easy to want to give up. Oftentimes, the energy and effort it takes to be a good wife, maintain a job and raise children seems like futile work with few rewards. Again, older and mature women have proof that what God established for the family has many rewards that pay countless dividends.

Unfortunately, I believe the reason we lack sufficient role models and mentors for women in the body of Christ is simple. Church, civic, and other leaders in society have not given this essential earth assignment the proper recognition. In the many churches I have observed, I do not see an emphasis placed on nurturing godly mentors. I do see much time given to other gifts, i.e., hospitality, worship, youth and missions.

By his words, teachings and actions; Jesus mentored adults so that they could in turn be great husbands, parents, grandparents, civic leaders, caregivers, businessmen and more. He used his mentoring program—called discipleship, to transform the world. I wonder if we could not do the same?.

I truly believe in mentoring youth. That is why I launched a character-development non-profit for youth and led it with excellence for nearly 12 years in Columbus, Ohio. However, I have now come to acknowledge the essential mandate to mobilize warrior women of worth who can carry the Titus II mandate to the body of Christ. Women are nurturers by nature, but we simply need to stir up the gift.

Women and girls are constantly bombarded with advertisements, online videos and magazines that project images of what appears to be the ideal life. They may look attractive and impressive on the outside, but what we cannot see is the hidden pain of misguided relationships, self-loathe and fears that plague those who are without God and who have no hope.

Don't be fooled by social media posts and "likes." People only post their dressed up personas. We see carefully cultivated images of pretty faces with people in nice homes, new cars, enjoying fancy vacations… while struggles and hardships aren't mentioned. Only the most flattering snapshots are posted.

It doesn't make sense to compare ourselves to others, when we know what we see is not the whole story. Instead, we would make better use of our time by focusing on perfecting and promoting that confident and beautiful person God has called us to be.

If you are more impressed with what you see on television, and less impressed about you, it's time to take a closer look. None of us with kingdom purpose have time to waste listening to and watching lewd and pretentious behavior. Biblical wisdom can be found in II Corinthians 10:12 to help us break the comparison habit. I love the wisdom found in these words:

II Corinthians 10:12 & 13 (NIV): We do not dare to classify or compare ourselves with some who commend themselves. When they measure themselves by themselves and compare themselves with themselves, they are not wise.

We, however, will not boast beyond proper limits, but will confine our boasting to the field God has assigned to us, a field that reaches even to you.

There is value in filtering our thoughts to allow the main thing to remain the main thing. This is the way we water and nurture our "mind field" so that our rose gardens will blossom with beauty. When we do this, we have the mental capacity to mentor and enrich the lives of others.

I've been taught to replace every negative thought with two positive ones. Of course, at times people discount or ignore us. They rush by, avoiding eye contact, ignore our emails and texts. Don't let this get to you. You still have an assignment on your life to reach out to others. Always remember, you can make a difference in someone's life. Don't give out or give up.

There are times when we are simply expecting too much from others. Our feelings of rejection are rooted in being too critical of ourselves. Instead, we must take our ques from the word of God allowing His word to spur us to action. This is where constructive soul-searching begins. Are our efforts to share our story or the word of God being sabotaged by self-defeating thoughts? Be determined to evaluate every thought that does not line up with the word of God.

In college, I hung a sign on my dorm wall that read, "To Thine Own Self Be True." I knew I had a proclivity to be a people-pleaser. This was my reminder to truly evaluate my feelings rather than going along with every suggestion to please others. I've also learned along the way to truly evaluate what is good for my own physical and spiritual well-being.

Over the years, I have learned that women who truly value the word of God as their rule for faith and practice, find the courage to walk-away from old habits and toxic people. This is when true confidence begins to emerge. We can then find freedom to articulate our true convictions and values without being ashamed or afraid of what others might think or say. Having mentoring moments with caring and compassionate confidants can be helpful during times when we need reassurance. None of us have all the answers, all the time.

PERSPECTIVE ON CONFIDENCE

Not long after I married my husband, I asked him what he considered to be sexy in a woman. I had some thoughts of my own, but I wanted to hear a man's perspective—especially his. He did not mention hair, skin-color, eyes, a shapely-figure or attire. To my surprise, he simply said, "Confidence."

I thought how intriguing... and was happy that I asked because it changed my perspective on "sexy." To this day, the word "confidence" resonates with me as a core value that causes a woman to stand out.

What images come to mind when you think of the word "confidence?" Perhaps you visualize a woman smiling in a way that signals trustworthiness and friendship. Her countenance is radiant and welcoming as she listens and actively engages in conversation. She looks happy, comfortable, and self-assured. She is perhaps well-dressed—or maybe she's wearing jeans with a comfy top. But, one thing that I feel pretty certain of is—her eyes are gleaming with joy and her countenance is vibrant and full of light.

The word of God tells us that in God, there is no darkness at all. Being and looking confident isn't really about what you wear on the outside, but the glow that beams from the inside. For the kingdom woman, confidence goes hand-in-hand with "class" and "credibility." These are the tangible, stand out qualities of a self-aware woman of God. I believe all three are "keys to competence" for the "get noticed" woman. Packaged together in the physical realm, these qualities attract and draw others to the Christ within.

Women can appear confident, but lack the gracious and accommodating spirit of a self-assured person. People who are self-absorbed and show signs of disinterest are unattractive to those around them. Their detached attitude repels rather than attracts. Let's define the terms I just mentioned. They are key to understanding the essence of the get noticed woman.

- Confidence—A radiant countenance marked by a look of self-assuredness.

- Class—A distinctive look of elegance punctuated by gracious behavior.

- Credibility—A character trait that is reputable and trustworthy; marked by authenticity, respect, and honor.

When these three competencies are embodied in a woman's demeanor, people are drawn to that "something special." Her eyes may seem to glimmer with confidence, and her radiant countenance is a beauty to behold. This notable attraction draws attention to her "gift package," which is the essence of what she brings to the world. When a woman knows her value, it shows in her eyes and demeanor. When she is not just born again, but, has a true and vital *relationship* with her Lord and Savior, Jesus Christ—her countenance reflects the glory of the Lord.

I asked one of our sons-in-laws what he believes makes a woman attractive and beautiful? He said, "First of all, a praying woman; there is something very attractive about a woman who prays for her man." Secondly, he said, "Beautiful eyes and smile; these two physical attributes never change with time." Thirdly, he said, "A sense of humor; laughter cures almost anything." There you have it—points of view from very astute and level-headed men on beauty and attractiveness.

"Get Noticed" is a paradigm shift for many, and some may view the title as a theme for encouraging women to be self-centered attention seekers. Nothing could be further from the truth. Instead, I am sharing a concept that we need to grasp and embrace. I envision a network of women worldwide who embody this truth. A total transformation taking place with women of God who once struggled with fear, self-doubt, and uncertainties; now holding the keys of transformation.

Recognized or unrecognized, greatness is within us all. Perhaps you may suffer from a physical or mental challenge. We all have limitations of some sort. However, focusing on our strengths and potential will allow us to exceed expectations.

SUFFERING IN SILENCE

Many women were taught to "keep quiet, mind your own business, and mind your manners." They were told this with no further information regarding the how of doing this. In my childhood, being confident was often misperceived as being arrogant and "out of place." So, girls learned to be reticent and live on the side-lines. As I mentioned earlier, being constantly told "it's not lady-like to be vocal and opinionated," left a gaping hole in my self-esteem.

I'll never forget living in Washington, D.C.—how insecure I felt when the human resources manager on my first job assignment approached me about where I'd like to live in the area. I was shy and didn't speak up, so she gave me directions to a section of town where I could find housing.

Even though I worked with mostly Caucasian women, curiously enough, I found myself standing in a bus line with mostly African-American employees, while other bus lines had mostly Caucasians. She had placed me where she thought I belonged.

I eventually found a nice apartment, but my lack of sophistication and inability to speak up for myself limited my choices and put my fate in someone else's hands. Perhaps if I had been schooled differently and had the sophistication to be more decisive, I would have at least had the confidence to ask more questions so that I could shop around. Perhaps I would have discovered an apartment I liked much more than the one I settled into.

This often happens in life. We may have the holy spirit implanted within and the intelligence to match, however, when we look unsure of ourselves and remain silent, those in power place us where they *think* we belong.

Many of us have tried to "play by the rules" by being quiet and demure; while deep inside we've been screaming, "I'm talented too! Why am I being overlooked and ignored?" There are many reasons—it's not always gender, race, age or talent.

We all need opportunities to be heard; however, we must be prepared when those opportunities come knocking. Unfortunately, being quiet, reticent and unsure does little to help us advance in a competitive world.

As an image coach and later as an ordained minister, I found that women use "hidden language" to couch emotional pain. They become invisible when they prefer not to be involved and productive.

When we are emotionally drained and unhealthy, we attract the wrong friends and romantic partners—then life moves into a downward spin. Emotional pain can cause a woman to do irrational things. Some have suddenly quit a job and even a marriage—just because they are—"fed up."

Isn't it interesting to note that when a woman isn't happy, it shows on her face? No amount of make-up can hide the pain inside. It is no secret that women suffer disproportionately to men when it comes to emotional pain and body image. Here are few revealing statistics:

Fact #1 – The average height of a woman in the U.S. is approximately 5-feet-4-inches, and the average weight is about 163 pounds. These figures vary greatly throughout the world due to differences in nutrition and prenatal care. Knowing the statistics, most women who feel "abnormal" are in reality quite normal.

Fact #2 – Over 90% of all cases of eating disorders occur in women, and nearly seven million women in the U.S. currently suffer from anorexia nervosa or bulimia.

These statistics are truly eye-opening. Being unhealthy or feeling uncomfortable because of weight issues challenges millions of American women. Hiding just simply doesn't work. Facing the person in the mirror will not only work for you, but, your example may be a catalyst to help others face their demons.

One of the areas that consistently captures a woman's attention is her body shape and appearance. For this reason, health and wellness is key to building a sense of personal well-being. Knowledge is indeed power, enabling us to do and be more. Taking a brief look at this "insider secret" to physical health and well-being can be transformative. When we know we are functioning at optimal levels physically and nutritionally, even our mental state is rejuvenated. Let's evaluate where we stand.

HEALTH, WELLNESS & BODY IMAGE

Do you feel confident about the state of your health, wellness and body image? Do you find yourself preoccupied with the next diet—or figuring out how to cheat the bathroom scale? My awakening came in modeling school when I could no longer hide behind a shirt dress. One of my daily assignments was to become totally comfortable with me—the woman in the mirror.

Unfortunately, the answer to health, wellness, and being happy with your body image doesn't begin with low-fat foods and diet drinks. That's like popping breath mints all day when you simply need to brush your teeth! Some resort to cosmetic surgery and tummy tucks which are not only risky, but they do not always offer the longed-for solution. The weight can come back. The surgery can be botched. It stands to reason that learning to live healthy is a much better option.

It is never too late to be what you might have become.
—George Eliot

Let's face it—being healthy is a key to having a confident self-image. Women struggle with body image every day. Wouldn't it be amazing if we would act on what we know to be true? We would live longer and lead more fulfilling lives. Next, I want to share some basic guidelines to health, wellness, and beauty to discover the "fab" in our fabulous without the worry, guilt, and regret.

OPTIMAL HEALTH & WELLNESS

You can't be optimally healthy without exercise. We all know that a healthy diet and exercise go hand in hand. There are many online health and fitness advisories to help women stay in touch with looking and feeling their best. You will find many reputable options online. Some focus on particular pre-existing conditions. Be prayerful and select the one or ones you believe right for you.

Major studies show that 60-90 minutes of exercise is best at least 3 or 4 days per week for healthy individuals. Dr. Joseph M. Mercola, a licensed physician, surgeon and health expert recommends at least 30-minutes of exercise daily to experience weight loss benefits. He also offers the following exercise tips:

- If you're on medication, under doctors' care or have certain physical limitations, consult your physician first before beginning a new exercise plan.

- Break your routine into short breaks for maximum effectiveness called interval training (sprints) with endurance cardio training (running).

- Do weight-training if you can't run or don't have the right surface for cycling.

- Once you have normalized your weight and insulin levels, you may only need to exercise only three or four times per week.

- Your intensity should be at the level that allows you to talk to someone next to you. If you can't carry-on a conversation, you've gone too far and should decrease the intensity.

MAKING HEALTHY FOOD CHOICES

To look and feel your best remains a matter of discipline. Reviewing your food choices is the next step to optimal health. This anti-aging and anti-disease statement rings very true:

Every vital nutrient must be available within the body – for the support of the cell –All of the time.
The Code of Life by Dr. Ronald Drucker

The key to basic nutritional health is a diet of whole, nutritious, and live foods, rather than the processed ones found in boxes and cans on grocery store shelves. As we study current trends in food production, we find that the U.S. agricultural industry permits and introduces numerous antibiotics, pesticides, genetically-engineered ingredients, hormones, and countless drugs into our food supply.

When purchasing groceries from a typical supermarket, many fruits and vegetables are unhealthy because of chemical sprays, wax and other treatments to make them look appetizing. Although some chemicals have been banned in other countries, the FDA in the USA continue to permit chemical sprays, etc. Rinsing and soaking all fresh fruits and vegetables with a mixture of one-eighth cup white-vinegar per gallon of water helps to remove toxic sprays and chemicals.

Shopping at local farm-markets ensures healthy produce, supports local industry and the production of humanely-raised animal products. One way you might be able to find quality food is by logging onto www.localHarvest.org, and enter your zip code to find markets in your area. More tips to remember when shopping for health-promoting foods:

- Contains no growth-hormones, antibiotics, or other drugs.

- Contains no artificial ingredients or chemical preservatives.

- Is not genetically modified and is fresh (if you must choose between wilted organic produce, and fresh conventional produce, the latter may be the better option).

- Does not come from a factory farm that uses grains and animal byproducts... or chicken and eggs with growth-hormones, antibiotics and drugs, but is grown by the laws-of-nature with animals fed their native diets and free-range access to outdoors.

- Is grown in a sustainable way... using minimal amounts of water, protecting the soil from burnout, and turning animal wastes into natural fertilizers instead of environmental pollutants.

If the food meets these criteria, it is most likely a wise choice, and would fall under the designation of "real food." Keep in mind that reclaiming your kitchen is part of healthful living, so you know exactly what you're putting in your body.
—Optimize Your Health, Dr. Joseph Mercola

Other helpful tips to optimize your health and normalize your weight—especially during this challenging time when globally, we have been challenged by a life-threatening COVID pandemic. Make sure you take health promoting vitamins supplements to strengthen your immune system. In particular, make certain you are getting your minimal daily requirement of vitamin C, D3 and zinc. Also do the following:

- Address emotional traumas.

- Get exposure to sunlight to get enough vitamin D.

- Drink only pure water.

- Avoid all toxins.

- Eat the right fats.

- Eat right for your blood type.

- Eat raw foods.

- Control your insulin and leptin levels.

- Exercise regularly.

- Get proper sleep and rest.

WHAT IS A CLASSY, INFLUENTIAL KINGDOM WOMAN?

Being confident, as well as emotionally and physically healthy requires intentional and disciplined work. What's more, the importance of improving yourself never ends. When a young woman graduates from high school or college, she needs to look and feel her best to compete in the marketplace.

Getting married and preparing to rear children or grandchildren require a whole new skill set. When aging and coping with physical and mental changes, we require yet another skill set to avoid feelings of depression and hopelessness as our bodies and energy level change.

We never reach a place where we can relax and say, "I've got it." Each new day presents a different set of challenges physically, mentally and nutritionally to feel confident and vital. To do this, it is important to be surrounded with energetic and enthusiastic people who are inspirational and encouraging.

Finding like-minded women you admire, can learn from and that inspire personal, professional and spiritual growth is essential to maintaining mental health. It is often said that we can gage a person's lifestyle by their 5 closest friends. Who are your spiritual, professional and personal mentors in life? Growth requires an upgrade. If you find that stagnation is plaguing you, it may be time to widen your circle of friends and associates.

I love the growth that can happen when women connect and begin to learn from the education and experiences of others. The scripture speaks of "iron sharpening iron" in Proverbs 27:17. This scripture is specifically speaking of influence. When a kingdom person is gracious—smiles—shares a gift of love; this causes the countenance of his or her friend to light up.

The root of the word "class" comes from the Latin word *classius*, meaning "first in rank." I often speak of a woman with "class" as one with a distinctive look of elegance, punctuated by gracious behavior.

Classy, confident kingdom women empower and draw other women because of the caring and nurturing spirit of Christ that lives within them. A page in my journal says, "Be the reason someone smiles today." This is the power of "influence." They show signs of a healthy kind of influence that does not come with pretentious motives—only to give life—body soul and spirit.

While writing this book, I asked a few women, "What does a classy kingdom woman look like? How would you describe her—how does she behave?" One person said the word "classy" is outdated. Another commented that we need to see more of the characteristics of this type of woman! Another person said this type of person would be charismatic with grace and compassion. I like that!

Proverbs also speaks of *unhealthy* influences. Of course, they are countless in number. Here are a few:

- My son, give me your heart and let your eyes observe my ways; for a whore is a deep ditch; and a strange woman is a narrow pit. (Prov. 23:27)

- Who has redness of eyes? They that tarry long at the wine; …at the last will bite like a serpent… your eyes shall behold strange women and your heart shall utter perverse things. (Prov. 23: 30-33)

- Two things do I require of thee…remove far from me vanity and lies: give me neither poverty nor riches; feed me with food convenient for me: Let I be full, and deny thee, and say, "Who is the Lord?" Or lest I be poor, and steal, and take the name of my God in vain. (Prov. 30:7-9)

A classy kingdom woman is intentional about being tactful, tolerant and discreet. She does not boast and is not prideful. She is conscious of what is appropriate and in good taste. She is "first in rank," not only in her appearance but in her behavior and performance on the job. She knows when to speak and when to remain silent. She is aware of the rules of decorum and understands foundational keys to building positive relationships. She is careful to maintain a welcoming attitude even in difficult social situations.

While many of the qualities our mothers and grandmothers taught us about being polite, decent, and respectful have been trampled at the expense of being politically correct, kingdom women get noticed as men and men of excellence because the spirit of Christ outlives and outshines every dogma designed by man. This means, we are the role models our children and grandchildren need to make know the character of Christ. As Titus II teachers and examples—may we never abandon our post as "princess warriors," mentors and vanguards of dignity and truth.

SPIRITUAL CHARACTERISTICS OF "THE GET NOTICED WOMAN"

A woman of influence and class will chart her course with her eyes fixed on excellence. She does this knowing that the success of today leads to greater achievements tomorrow—for her family, and for those who need a roadmap to follow. She is a realist. Her vision is cast not only by present achievements, but she also has the future in mind. She understands the significance of leaving a lasting legacy. She also understands the significance of not only doing all things well—but with excellence.

Women need and want to succeed. They deserve to receive recognition and rewards for their accomplishments. Yet, some have compromised their reputations and values to receive a shallow compliment or accolade. This is unfortunate. We shouldn't be pressured into submitting to ideologies that don't fit our belief system—especially in the realm of the spirit.

The stakes are too high for settling for less than our best. No one becomes a pro overnight. However, as my friend, psychologist Dr. Loleta Foster, says, "Intentional acts practiced with consistency can create extraordinary results."

Intentional acts of kindness are required to leave a lasting legacy. When I think of the word "kindness," I think of the fruit of the spirit as mentioned in Galatians. The first word mentioned as a fruit is the word "love." As motivational speaker and minister, Mike Murdock says, "The proof of love is the investment of time."

A woman who wants to accomplish great things must intentionally invest time and energy into the word of God. We can't love God without becoming acquainted with His message via His word. A woman of God is the personification and a representative of that message. She is not flamboyant nor arrogant, deliberately calling attention to herself. Instead, she commands attention because she radiates the life of Christ that is within.

A woman of excellence will take the time necessary to invest the time needed to cultivate qualities of honesty and integrity. At her core is the manifestation of the fruit of the spirit. The fruit of the spirit is clearly named and defined in Galatians 5:22-25. A paraphrased version is outlined below:

"But the fruit of the spirit is love, joy, peace, longsuffering, gentleness, goodness, faith, meekness, temperance: against these there is no law. And those who belong to Christ have crucified (considered dead) the flesh with the affections and desires of the flesh. If we live in the spirit, let us also walk in the spirit."

Fruit is the outgrowth of a seed. The seed that germinates and produces fruit is a God-given gift—the spirit from on high as first received on the day of Pentecost—the holy spirit. As we review the context of this passage, it is interesting to note that there is a perpetual war going on between the life of the flesh and the spirit. (Galatians 5:16 &17). The daily actions and mindset of the kingdom woman determines the final outcome.

Some of the more recognizable works of the flesh listed in Galatians 5:19 are: adultery, fornication, uncleanness, lasciviousness (sensuality), idolatry, witchcraft, hatred, wrath, strife, heresies, envying, murders, drunkenness and more. It says that those who do such things will not enter the kingdom of God.

The get noticed woman stands out as notable because she has disciplined her life to walk in the spirit rather than to submit to living by the whims of her flesh. She is a spirit-led woman. She is a worthy role model and mentor to disciple and mentor others.

QUALITIES OF THE GET NOTICED WOMAN

She is mature, confident and disciplined; managing her affairs with excellence. Because of these qualities, she is a woman of power and influence. Just as the honey bee is attracted to nectar from the fruit of the vine; the fruit of the spirit when manifested encourages, draws and is influential in nature.

Some of her prominent qualities and characteristics are listed here:

- She is considerate and gracious while being careful not to gossip or belittle others.

- She is influential and respected by her peers and those who know her.

- She is not arrogant; but respectful to her parents all the days of her life—understanding that the word of God insures long life when we do so.

- She respects and honors her elders and those who are in authority—especially in the church and in the body of Christ.

- She protects her reputation by carefully choosing friends and associates.

- She is gracious and genuinely accepts others no matter their age, status or ethnicity.

- She is tactful and uses discretion when handling conflict and challenging situations.

- She is honest and ethical and doesn't compromise her morals or integrity for monetary gain.

- She is loyal and discreet in keeping confidences.

- She is empathetic, shows generosity and is not selfish.

- She is comfortable using the rules of manners and etiquette to show respect and build meaningful relationships.

Although I've been blessed with countless numbers of classy, kingdom women who have served as role models in my life, I am always looking for a good example to follow. I never want to be comfortable with where I am mentally, physically or spiritually. I consistently place myself in learning situations so I can be challenged to grow.

CREDIBILITY COUNTS

A woman of excellence is also credible—it's part of the package. The fruit of the spirit demands that she is reputable and trustworthy, meriting respect. She is proactive about protecting her reputation by choosing her friends and associates wisely. Even when she happens to miss the mark, she strives to improve and never settles for less.

Credibility will wrestle down jealousy and other negative behaviors that successful and attractive women face. There are "haters" in families, on jobs and in the grocery store. Women must learn to "hold their own" and do it with dignity, which is part of carrying a credible name and reputation.

A confident and classy woman is a winner on the playing field of life. She can keep her head together and dodge the punches when necessary. She is not a pretender, a cheat or a liar. Authenticity is important to her. She not only desires to be true to herself, but to others.

I believe having a conversation about integrity is essential for "the get noticed woman." It's easy to tell ourselves we are authentic persons. But, with all the cultural hype created to target women, we must do a mental check-up to make sure we are not being subtlety and negatively influenced by others.

Many years ago, I had a friend whose hard working and ingenious husband landed a high paying job because he was a self-taught engineer. He created a fake resume with bogus credentials and was hired for a prestigious position. When they discovered he falsified his background information, he lost his job; eventually his family, and of course, his upstanding reputation.

We can probably all share a similar story from personal experience. But if we are not careful, we can lie to ourselves when we receive a compliment or two about our skills and talent, and actually believe we are something that we are not.

Being honest with ourselves and others will help keep our lives free from scandal and scandalous people. No matter our income or status in life, the feminine traits of confidence, class, and credibility are my three "keys to competence" for get noticed women. These qualities help kingdom women stay on top of their game.

This, of course, doesn't mean she won't make mistakes and encounter difficulties along the way. However, when we live with care and consideration of others, occasional blunders will be easily forgiven. People trust us to handle important business. Our desire to do things with excellence and to be a positive influence will have a far-reaching ripple effect extending beyond our immediate circle, impacting our communities and those we know and serve.

MY CORE VALUES

Spiritual disciplines are the foundation keys to building ethical and credible behavior. As I mentioned before, my core values and disciplines as a woman of God bring balance and stability to my life.

I love Romans 13:9 (NIV) which serves as one of my foundational scriptures to live by:

"...the commandments are summed up in this one rule: "Love your neighbor as yourself." Love does no harm to its neighbor. Therefore love is the fulfillment of the law."

How amazing is this. A summary of the most potent laws of scripture entails loving our neighbor as ourselves. Upon reflection and consideration, the question to be asked becomes: How well am I doing at loving myself so that I don't shortchange others?

The whole study of image and etiquette presupposes that self-care enables us to be more caring and respectful to and for others. Therefore, building a confident woman helps to prepare and qualify nurturing others—who in turn beautify the world with their fragrance.

This is the very nature of the word "influence." To have influence simply means to have an impact or effect on others. An influential kingdom person inspires goodness, provides guidance and releases courage to do more and be more.

My friend, Evangelist Evon Hughes passed away in an auto accident coming home from midnight prayer on New Year's day, January 1st, 2019. I will never forget her gift to me at my second ordination on December 6, 2016.

We were together at Christian Provision Ministries in Sanford, N. Carolina when she presented me with a gift basket. In the basket was a gift I will always treasure. She wrote on a white candle—from the wick to the base: *"Light on assignment... Matthew 5:14-16."* The NIV translation reads like this:

> *You are the light of the world. A city on a hill cannot be hidden. Neither do people light a lamp and put it under a bowl. Instead, they put it on its stand, and it gives light to everyone in the house. In the same way, let your light shine before men, that they may see your good deeds and praise your Father in heaven.*

In essence—not only are we called to place our lights on a candlestick—we are called to be *influential* in this world. Our lives have significance. Our good works should be known, seen and impactful so that our Father gets the glory. We are not prideful or boastful; however, we make a difference.

When we look up the word "influential" in the dictionary, we see that it can be defined as: high-ranking, powerful, significant, leading, prominent, instrumental, forceful, persuasive, dominant and important. Do you see yourself in this way?

This book was written so that we can be renewed, reformed, transformed and reclaimed for the kingdom. We've been living in hog country too long. It's time to **get noticed**!

Evon left me a powerful gift. She reminded me—fortified my calling and vision. She recommissioned me to do what God placed me here to do—in my particular realm of talent and giftedness. Indeed, this was a prophetic reminder of the assignment God has placed on my life—to be an influential light.

As lights on assignment, God's desire is that we shine unimpeded. Matthew 6:22 says that the light of the body is the eye—and that if our eye is single (without defect) our whole body will be full of light. How powerful is that! There is no mention of the size of our hips or breasts. There is no mention of our skin color or our national origin. So how did we get preoccupied with mental gymnastics that "make no never-mind to God?"

That which we are thinking, believing and feeling is reflected in our eyes. Lives are changed when we reflect God's glory. When there is doubt, worry or shame—this is what our eyes reflect. A daily prayerful, disciplined lifestyle is required. Although the Holy Spirit resides within every believer—we daily make a choice to let it shine by our thoughts and actions.

In my personal life, I try to take good care of me so that not only am I fulfilled and whole, but so that I can be a contributing factor to encourage and inspire others. I rely on my spiritual disciplines to sustain and protect me from fear, anxiety, and hopelessness. They are as follows:

- Begin the day with prayer and meditation. I call this "me time."

- Count my blessings and read the word of God for guidance, encouragement and strength.

- Be compassionate, considerate and forgiving, remembering how God extends the same to me.

- Negative self-talk is an enemy. Replace each negative "I can't" with "I can." Don't dwell on my mistakes or those of others. They have passed and are in the past.

- We have all made mistakes and will continue to make them. Commit to forget and to forgive.

- Be deliberate about protecting my eyes, ears, and thoughts from social media, music, movies and environments that can potentially contaminate my mind, heart and spirit. I try to investigate the source. I love jazz—and I love to dance, however, I try to ask myself—do the words of the song or amusement have a negative impact on my thinking or my spirit?

- Be prayerful and selective about friends and associates. If we do not enjoy mutual respect, we cannot be productive in the work of the kingdom. Negative people can stunt your personal and spiritual growth.

- Choose mentors who walk in wisdom and are open to mutual accountability.

- Be protective about your environment; as well as the voices and media you allow to enter your eye and ear gateways. Try to surround yourself with people who value your voice, gifts and talents.

Spiritual disciplines ingrained in one's life provide core values upon which one can build strong character. When a woman is secure and grounded in her personal and spiritual life, she will provide a good example for others as a light in the kingdom.

I have a plaque sitting on my desk that reads, "Behind every great woman is a lot of other great women." The women who influenced my life to the greatest and most meaningful extent have strong spiritual values.

My mother and grandmother were the greatest influencers in my life, weaving threads of faith, character, courage, honesty and endurance in the fabric of my being. Without their example, I could not have withstood the adversity life brought my way.

I have had many mentors and teachers in my lifetime. I've learned that although much has been gained from these experiences over time, the only flawless example is Christ. The Apostle Paul knew this and expressed his sentiments in this way in I Corinthians 11:1 (NIV): Follow my example, as I follow the example of Christ. Paul's life was influenced and changed by men and women who followed Christ. From their examples, he then taught and mentored Timothy.

Kingdom women today have the same mandate to follow after Christ and to then mentor those who are meek and desire to live godly in Christ. To become an influential role model, we must become students of the word of God, which will provide guidance and instruction to teach us the ways of God.

Not only is it important to learn but, we must abide in the faith. To abide means to be unwavering; to stay fixed on a goal through discipline and study. As we are taught in II Timothy 2:15, we must be workmen that have no need to be ashamed of our workmanship.

Paul taught Timothy what God had revealed to him in the spirit. He scripted that which was to come. I believe those days he spoke of then, have already arrived:

I Timothy 4:1:
The Spirit clearly says that in later times, some will abandon the faith and follow deceiving spirits and things taught by demons. Such teachings come through hypocritical liars...they forbid people to marry and order them to abstain from certain foods, which God created to be received with thanksgiving... nothing is to be rejected if it is received with thanksgiving, because it is consecrated by the word of God and prayer.

Verse 12: Don't let anyone look down on you because you are young, but set an example for the believers in speech, in life, in love, in faith and in purity.

Verse 13: Until I come, devote yourself to public reading of Scripture, to preaching and to teaching.

Do not neglect your gift (remember that Paul is writing to his mentee Timothy), which was given you through prophetic message when the body of elders laid their hands on you.

Be diligent in these matters; give yourself wholly to them, so that everyone may see your progress.

Watch your life and doctrine closely. Persevere in them, because if you do, you will save both yourself and your hearers.

Understand the word "if" used here. Not everyone has or will be a disciple; nor will everyone choose to be a kingdom influencer. It is a choice.

The Get Noticed Woman is a kingdom influencer by choice. She has chosen to pursue the excellence that is in Christ Jesus and treasure this as her greatest prize. II Corinthians 4:7 says, metaphorically, that we have this treasure in "jars of clay" or earthen vessels that the excellence we carry is from God and not of us.

She is not compromised or conflicted by "political correctness." Her thoughts and actions are not influenced by trends and the philosophies bantered about by social media and the like. Her heart is fixed on the truth of the word of God as her source for faith and practice.

Just as the apostles suffered persecution in Acts 5:18, we too must endure the discomfort of rejection and malicious behavior. They were incarcerated by unbelieving Sadducees (Jewish scholars & theologians remaining fixed on religious laws) who verbally and physically attacked them. As the saints of God prayed, the angel of the Lord opened the prison doors by night and told them to, "Go, stand and speak in the temple to the people, all the words of this life."

Acts 5:28 says that Peter and the other disciples defied the mandate passed down to them by the authorities. Their response to their unbelieving accusers was: "We ought to obey God rather than men."

The "get noticed woman" is not a wimp wearing designer jeans. She must be strong in the Lord and in the power of his might. She does not boast of herself but, but knows the excellence of the power of Christ Jesus within.

By now, you know that when God created you in your mother's womb, he had a plan for you. If you are not clear as to how or where to begin your journey of discovery; I have listed some tips for you:

- Make a concerted effort to identify what you're good at. What are you passionate about?

- Write your mission and vision statement: What problem would you like to solve that will make a difference in the world? What obstacles can you anticipate? How will you overcome them?

- What audience will you target and why?

- Identify partners and mentors to help support you and to hold you accountable.

- Make a list of two and five-year goals. How will you accomplish your goals?

- What resources do you need to succeed... education, finances, training?

- Put a plan in place and make it happen. Write the vision and make it plain. Habakkuk 2:2

Recently, I have been inspired to launch the Get Noticed Academy, LLC and Sister-friend Circles to support the dreams women carry. The Academy offers Pathways 2 Prayer so that kingdom women can deepen their relationships with the heavenly Father. As we sit with Him and inquire, He will speak to us regarding our God-given assignment on the earth. I call this "me time." This one addition to our daily discipline—making prayer our early morning priority can be life changing.

In addition, you will find on the Academy website, my Leadership Institute, which will provide coaching and mentoring opportunities. When enrolled in the Institute, individuals will engage in a 4 step S.T.A.R.R. initiative.

The STARR initiative looks like this: Design a STRATEGY—TARGET your audience—make an ACTION plan—Gather your RESOURCES and finally, share your RESULTS. Our academy can be your one stop shop for getting on a new path to being all God called you to be.

I've kept this poem in my book of affirmations for many years. I want to share it with you in hopes that it will be inspiring to you—as it still is to me, each time I read it.

"LIVE EACH DAY TO THE FULLEST"
By S. A. Payer
Get the most from each hour, each day, and each age of your life.
Then you can look forward with confidence, and back without regrets.
Be yourself—but be your best self.
Dare to be different and to follow your own star.
And don't be afraid to be happy.
Enjoy what is beautiful. Love with all your heart and soul.
Believe that those you love, love you.
Forget what you have done for your friends.
Remember what they have done for you.
Disregard what the world owes you and concentrate on
what you owe the world.

However, I do not agree. I believe there are only two categories of women—believer and unbeliever. God gave kingdom women extraordinary super powers—wonder woman on steroids. That means, other women have excuses. Kingdom women do not. What is true is that kingdom women are more seriously imprisoned by limiting thoughts, low self-esteem and low ambition than by written laws or injustices imposed upon us.

God gave us liberty through Christ Jesus to be what He has called us to be when we were in our mother's wombs. God says in His word that we were created in His likeness. As Psalm 71 says—you are a wonder!

Psalm 71:6-9 paraphrased:
"By thee (Oh God) have I been brought forth from the womb: you are
He that took me out of my mother's bowels (womb): my praise shall
continually be of you. I am as a wonder unto many; but you are my
strong refuge. Let my mouth be filled with your praise and with your
honor all the day. Cast me not off in the time of old age;
forsake me not when my strength begins to fail."

When a woman truly begins to realize her God-given potential; her gender, race, ethnic background, age and economic status will not impede her progress, nor be a distraction. Not to imply that all the many prejudices kingdom women face are not real; however, the will to win can supersede all.

In her book, *A Return to Love: Reflections on the Principles of 'A Course in Miracles'*, Marianne Williamson makes this statement:

> *"We ask ourselves, 'Who am I to be brilliant, gorgeous, talented, and fabulous?' Actually, who are you not to be? You are a child of God. Playing small does not serve the world. There is nothing enlightened about shrinking so that other people won't feel insecure around you. We are all meant to shine, as children do. We were born to make manifest the glory of God that is within us. It's not just in some of us; it's in everyone. And as we let our own light shine, we unconsciously give other people permission to do the same. As we are liberated from our own fear, our presence automatically liberates others."*

I have a suggestion… remove yourself from the company of those who do not support your dreams and begin to surround yourself with women and men who literally believe what the word of God says about you.

Challenging? Yes, but, I believe you can do this. You owe it to yourself to live this way. As you become more familiar with your feminine assets—your "gift package" as outlined in these pages, you will be free to embrace the brilliance that is YOU!

You are fearfully (awesomely) and wonderfully made. God has assured you that you can meet life's challenges with power and His word. You are gifted with super-natural abilities. No longer do you need to languish in the shadows. It's your turn to emerge from obscurity; to shine your light into the darkness of this world so that men and women can see your good works and glorify your Father in heaven.

My mentor, Nan Leaptrott, my lifelong mentor who helped bring my career to fruition, is a true example of a "get noticed woman." She wrote a tribute to me for a recent birthday. It really touched my heart. I want to share a portion of it here with you:

A saint crosses our path perhaps but once. You will not find her etched in a stain glass window, not living a sterile, uneventful life. Rather, you will find her giving and living her best self. Her love you can always trust. How do I know? I've met such a soul. Her name is Brenda Joyce Johnson.

Your life is like a beautiful woven tapestry... stitched into your tapestry is a deep spiritual charm. You live your life in elegant ways. You spread joy all around. You display great courage and inner strength.

Yes, Brenda, your life is a beautiful tapestry, one to be treasured.
–Nan Leaptrott, President, Global Business Consultants

I share this not to boast, but simply to say that I believe life is circular. What is shared with others comes back to you. And as I mentioned in another chapter—you cast your bread upon the waters and it will come back buttered—I promise. What you share with others will return to you in unimaginable ways.

I will forever cherish Nan, but, to know that I have also made a contribution to her life is icing on my cake with strawberries and ice cream on top. This is the essence of the get noticed woman—standing up and out so that God will ultimately get the glory.

Remember that you are not an afterthought. God birthed you into the kingdom by way of His spirit—so that you would bear fruit and impact the lives of others.

I have claimed this scripture as my "legacy theme." Psalm 71: 17 & 18 says this:

"Oh God, you have taught me from my youth: and because of this, I have declared your wondrous works. Now, when I am old and gray headed, O God, forsake me not, until I have showed your strength unto this generation, and your power to everyone that is to come."

This was God's original intent. It's called—pass it on. God so loved that He gave, and then, we do the same. He empowered us so that we can give good gifts—springing up to new life both in the natural and in the spirit.

Could it be that you are the most majestic and beloved star in the universe of God's creation? The universe is everything we can see, touch, feel and experience. After all, he has counted every hair on your head. He walks and talks with you. He sent his son to die for you. He crowned you with the majesty of His glory. He said that you are the apple of his eye—His workmanship created in Christ Jesus unto good works. As if that was not enough, He made you the light of the world—a city that cannot be hid.

The woman that you are and the one He created you to be should be one and the same. So shine, beautiful lady—shine. It's time for you to put on your Esther robe and Joan of Arc armor so you can fight the good fight of faith. It's time kingdom woman to get noticed!

Now also when I am old and gray headed, O God, forsake me not, until I have showed your strength unto this generation, and your power to everyone that is to come.

If I can be of service to you, your business, church or organization as a speaker, mentor or coach, please contact me. My email address is: bjetiquettecoach@gmail.com or visit my website: www.getnoticedacademy.com.